The Employer's Guide to
Grievance &
Discipline
Procedures

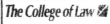
The Employer's Guide to
Grievance &
Discipline
Procedures

Identifying, addressing and
investigating employee misconduct

Mike Parkin

KOGAN
PAGE

London and Philadelphia

First published in Great Britain and the United States in 2009 by Kogan Page Limited

120 Pentonville Road
London N1 9JN
United Kingdom
www.koganpage.com

525 South 4th Street, #241
Philadelphia PA 19147
USA

© Mike Parkin, 2009

The right of Mike Parkin to be identified as the author of this work has been asserted by him in accordance with the Copyright, Designs and Patents Act 1988.

ISBN 978 0 7494 5414 2

British Library Cataloguing-in-Publication Data

A CIP record for this book is available from the British Library.

Library of Congress Cataloging-in-Publication Data

Parkin, Mike.
    The employer's guide to grievance and discipline procedures : identifying addressing and investigating employee misconduct / Mike Parkin.
        p. cm.
    Includes bibliographical references and index.
    ISBN 978-0-7494-5414-2
    1.   Labor discipline--United States.   I. Title.
    HF5549.5.L3P373 2008
    658.3'14--dc22
                            2008031335

Typeset by Saxon Graphics Ltd, Derby
Printed and bound in India by Replika Press Pvt Ltd

Contents

Foreword   *ix*

Introduction   **1**

1. **Setting the structure**   **9**
    The basics 9; Statutory dispute resolution procedures 10;
    ACAS code of practice on disciplinary and grievance
    procedures 13; Organizational policies and procedures 14;
    Misconduct and gross misconduct 14; The new provisions 16;
    The right to be accompanied 17; The small employer 19;
    'Interview' and 'hearing' 20

2. **Proactive discipline**   **22**
    The meaning of proactive 22; Policies and procedures 23;
    Recruitment and selection 24; Contracts and job
    descriptions 26; Induction 26; Probation 28; Informal
    discipline and setting standards 30; Management training 32;
    The 'last straw' 33; Difficult conversations 33;
    Concluding comments 35

3. **Reactive discipline**   **37**
    The philosophy 38; Reacting to misconduct 41; Reacting to
    gross misconduct 43; Formal action or not? 44; Conduct that
    occurs outside work 44

4. **Grievances** 47
   General comments 47; Why have grievance procedures? 48;
   Training and awareness 49; Drafting grievance procedures 49;
   Informal resolution 50; Formal procedure 51; Grievance
   investigations 51; Equal Pay Act 1970 52; Grievance raised
   during a discipline investigation 53; Grievance meetings 53;
   Written response 54; Appeals 56; Keeping records 57;
   Whistleblowing 58; Organizational review 61

5. **Suspensions** 62
   What suspension is 62; Suspension checklist 63; Special
   circumstances involving the complainant or victim 64;
   Suspension procedures 65; Responsibilities during
   suspension 66; Failure to follow terms of suspension 66;
   Resignation during suspension or investigation 67;
   'Persuading' an employee under investigation to resign 68;
   Constructive dismissal 68; Managing the grapevine 69;
   Reintroduction after suspension 70

6. **Capability** 72
   Potentially fair dismissal 72; General considerations 73; Initial
   action 74; Borderline cases 75; Capability checklist 76;
   Changes in working techniques 79; Denials of inadequate
   performance 80; Inadequate performance after promotion 80;
   Dismissal in capability cases 81; Capability and disability 83

7. **Special circumstances** 84
   Introduction 84; Definitions 85; Bullying 86; Third-party
   harassment 87; Sex and related forms of discrimination 87;
   Race 88; Disability 88; Burden of proof in discrimination
   cases 88; HIV and AIDS 89; Religious belief 89; Age
   discrimination 90; Criminal offences – organizational
   options 90; Failure to comply with instructions 92;
   Alcohol and drugs 92; Loss of driving licence 94; Trade union
   representatives 95; Data protection and human rights 95;
   Misuse of telephone, e-mail or internet 99

8. **Evidence and evidence gathering** 101
   What evidence is 101; Direct evidence 102; Corroboration 103;
   Circumstantial or indirect evidence 104; Admissibility and
   weight 104; Opinions 105; Hearsay evidence 105; Early
   complaint in cases of sexual harassment 105; Documentary
   evidence 106; The 'best evidence' rule 106; The burden of
   proof 106; Burden of proof in discrimination cases 107;
   The standard of proof 108; Presumptions 109; IT evidence 109;
   How to gather evidence 110; Drafting a chronology 110

9. **The investigation and the investigator**   114
   The investigation 114; The investigator 116; Using internal
   managers 116; External investigators 117; The investigator's
   skill set 117; Reflective practice 118; Body language 120; Time
   management 120; Problem-solving checklist 122;
   Mind-mapping 123; The terms of reference 123; Tools of the
   investigator 124; Using your chronology 124; Points to prove
   125; Tricks and devices 126; Custom and practice 127;
   Fraud investigations 128; CV fraud 129

10. **Interviewing**   130
    Introduction 130; Retracting a statement 131; 'Negative'
    statements 132; Anonymous witnesses 132; Communication
    and effective listening 134; Questioning techniques 135;
    Interview techniques 137; Traditional interviewing 137;
    WASP 138; The PEACE process 139; Witnesses 144;
    Suspects – the discipline interview 145; Note taking and
    statement writing 147; Interview checklist 147; Statement or
    notes checklist 147; Admissions and confessions 148;
    Recording interviews 150; Negotiation 150

11. **Report writing**   152
    Introduction 152; Discipline reports 153; Concepts 154;
    Techniques 155; Format 156; Starting the report 157;
    Mitigating circumstances 159; Extraneous issues 161;
    Plea-bargaining 161

12. **The discipline hearing**   162
    Introduction 162; The disciplinary officer 162; The panel 163;
    Administration 163; The hearing 164; Presenting the case 166;
    The role of the representative 167; Decision making 168;
    Problems in the hearing 169; Discipline appeals 170;
    Follow-up 172

13. **Case studies**   174
    Case study 1 – Simple discipline 175; Case study 2 – Internal
    grievance 178; Case study 3 – Grievance and discipline 180;
    Case study 4 – Discipline 183; Case study 5 – External
    complaint of sex discrimination 184; Case study 6 – Theft 187;
    General comments 188

14. **Pro forma documents**   190
    1 – Terms of reference 191; 2 – Example – suspension letter 193;
    3 – Example – suspension letter 194; 4 – Witness statement 195;
    5 – Example – notice of a disciplinary hearing 196; 6 – Example
    – dismissal letter 197; 7 – Example – 'not proven' letter 198;

8 – Example – 'final warning' letter 199; 9 – Example – notice of appeal hearing letter 200; 10 – Example – notice of result of appeal hearing 201; 11 – Example letter – notice of decision to invoke the formal procedures 202; 12 – Example letter – notice of initial review meeting 203; 13 – Example letter – notice of written warning or final written warning 204; 14 – Example letter – confirmation of dismissal (following previous warnings) 205

References   *206*

Index   *207*

Foreword

As a result of my review of employment dispute resolution in the UK, for the then Secretary of State for the Department of Trade and Industry, I have become very aware of the damage that conflicts at work can cause, especially when they continue for a long period of time. There is overwhelming evidence that disputes arising from work cost a great deal of time, money and stress to all the parties involved. For employees, the consequences of continuing conflict typically also include unemployment and, in many cases, ill health. Similarly, long standing disputes distract and often disrupt businesses. My review therefore made a series of recommendations which were collectively aimed at encouraging resolution of employment disputes as early as possible and ideally in the workplace itself rather than perpetuating the current system which tends to focus on the route to employment tribunals. From April 2009, resolving problems at work should become more straightforward. Employers and employees will have greater flexibility to chose how best to resolve their problems at work.

This useful book aims to give good, practical advice to managers as to best practise in the workplace in a wide range of employment situations. The author is clearly highly experienced and an undoubted expert in this field. His approach and style should mean that the book is easy to use and highly relevant to the modern working environment. I hope that these chapters, by the dissemination of good advice, may serve to help reduce and resolve disputes in the workplace. It is clear that many managers need more support to acquire people management skills, and this book should certainly help, and by doing so play its part in reducing conflict at work, which has such negative consequences for all concerned.

Michael J S Gibbons OBE
Author of Better Dispute Resolution, *DTI, March 2007*

Introduction

Even the most regulated and well-disciplined organization will face the prospect of discipline at some stage. It may be a simple case of poor attendance or it may be an allegation of sexual harassment. There could be some genuine confusion whether your employee is lazy and uncooperative or just unable to carry out their duties. If you are a manager you may be asked to take on the role of an independent investigator to look into allegations of expense account fiddles. The principal aim of this book is to help with all these difficult and potentially hazardous tasks.

Despite the fact that people have been in paid employment for many hundreds of years, it is only within my working life that concepts such as 'unfair dismissal', 'discrimination', harassment', 'redundancy', 'whistle-blowing' and 'formal grievance' have entered the employment arena. The rights and duties of the employer are now balanced by those of the employee.

Employers cannot take arbitrary action; their decisions need to be reasonable and fair. However, when tackled correctly, managers *can* deal with ill discipline and misconduct effectively. The position taken throughout this book is that all parties need to operate within the legal framework and context.

If you, the employer, find yourself in the throes of an employment tribunal it can prove to be a 'no-win' situation. Unless the claim can be proved to be malicious or vexatious it is unlikely costs will be awarded against the employee or ex-employee. Representation costs and management time will cost thousands – even if you win! Avoiding litigation is so much better. This book is aimed at developing the knowledge, skills and systems to deal with modern concepts of discipline within employment and with grievances raised by employees.

There comes a point in any business when enforcing discipline is necessary or a formal grievance must be addressed. A failure to deal with issues such as lateness, bullying and minor theft can have a major effect on the morale of other workers who see their colleagues getting away with ill discipline.

It is at these times when the tactics and techniques covered in the book are crucial. Your aim must be to get back to normal relations as soon as possible. If this is not possible and drastic action, such as a dismissal, is necessary, you should be able to achieve this in an effective and fair manner. While you can never prevent litigation you can put yourself in a favourable position to defend such action if it is taken. This book is not about dealing with employment tribunals claims, it is about seeking to deal with issues before this stage. My experience is that a well-documented and effective process before a dismissal often results in the claim being dropped.

IS DISCIPLINE NECESSARY?

An organization without discipline is a recipe for poor relationships, an unhappy working environment and imperfect cooperation between staff and management. It is an organization where a lack of respect, oppressive conduct, autocratic supervision, bullying, harassment and discrimination could be rife and unchecked. Production and quality control problems will be everyday issues and the employees are unlikely to show pride in their work.

Furthermore, it is likely that customer relations will deteriorate and so will orders. Recruitment will become a problem as the reputation of the company spreads, probably by the tales of ex-employees dismissed unfairly or those who have left after being treated badly. Remember, the best workers, those who can easily find employment, will leave first. Poor discipline often manifests itself in inadequate maintenance of equipment, sloppy paperwork, badly kept company vehicles, staff wasting hours playing computer games or gossiping, and employees spending too much time scanning the situations vacant pages of newspapers.

You will have a picture of the type of organization I refer to, whether it is a manufacturing company, an NHS Trust, a retailing outlet, service company, a local authority or even a professional office such as an accountancy or solicitors' practice. We shall look at the opposite of this particular scenario when we deal with _proactive discipline_ in Chapter 2.

WHAT ARE WE TRYING TO ACHIEVE?

The aim of this book is to provide a comprehensive guide to establishing a disciplined environment, dealing with discipline and grievances effectively yet sympathetically and setting up policies and procedures to ensure that companies follow best practice and legal requirements. Fairness and consistency are key words in a 'best practice' organization.

Smaller organizations are not expected to have the sophistication of larger employers but the basic principles are the same. The management skill set forming the backbone of the book is the same in any environment. The techniques will apply in most situations – interviewing, investigating, planning and communication skills are universal.

I want to reflect and reinforce the change brought about by the Michael Gibbons report _Better Dispute Resolution – A Review of Employment Dispute Resolution in Great Britain_ (2007), the new Employment Bill and the revised ACAS Codes of Practice.

HOW TO USE THIS BOOK

First, you could proceed from this Introduction to Chapter 1 and progress to the end of the book, in fact I hope you do. The topics covered are designed to be following sequentially although decisions to place certain topics one before the other have been taken arbitrarily. As you increase your knowledge and enhance your skills it will be necessary to refer to the case studies. These are designed to place the skills and techniques into a context.

Second, the book is designed to be used as a reference source to assist in any discipline or grievance situation you may find yourself involved in. It should be a source of advice, guidance, and I hope inspiration, to enable a manager to tackle the challenge with confidence.

In addition, the contents could be used as a textbook to support training of managers in investigating discipline issues. Remember, the skills and techniques covered in the following chapters are intended to build upon and not replace your own policies and procedures.

VICARIOUS LIABILITY

In some circumstances, employers can be held to be liable for the actions taken by their employees. For example, employers could be liable for construction workers failing to take adequate safety measures and operators of a school have been held to be liable for the actions of an employee sexually assaulting children at the school. Excessive injury caused by over-zealous club and restaurant door personnel is another example. At a less obvious level, employers could be liable for discriminatory practices carried out by their employees based on gender, race, and in fact almost any feature that creates the perception in some people's eyes that a person or a group is 'different'. The concept of *proactive discipline* will suggest how employers and managers can mitigate against these risks. In addition, several of the case studies tackle these areas.

Employers need to be aware that they could also be vicariously liable for action taken by their employees against other employees which cause physical, psychiatric or psychological injury, for example by negligence, assault, harassment or dangerous working practices. It is through selection, training, supervision and effective discipline that employers can have some control over the actions of their employees.

Finally, the Corporate Manslaughter and Corporate Homicide Act 2007 introduces new offences, making it possible for the government to prosecute companies and other organizations where there has been a gross failure, throughout the organization, in the management of health and safety with fatal consequences. This is an extreme risk but the existence of this law should serve to concentrate management focus on discipline.

HEALTH AND SAFETY

To move from the extreme to more everyday matters, complex health and safety requirements have been a creation of the latter third of the 20th century. The whole concept of health and safety requires a disciplined approach to work in the setting up and training in standard operating procedures. Misconduct relating to health and safety rules is quite common and features in many disciplinary actions, even dismissals. The taking of risks or 'cutting corners' has been commonplace in many industries, such as mining, construction and farming, often resulting in injury and loss of life. While some would argue that the 'health and safety' culture has progressed too far in society, it is clearly necessary in the employment arena.

Finally, health and safety has embraced issues such as work-related stress and other psychological and psychiatric illnesses.

'EMPLOYEE' AND 'WORKER'

Our focus throughout this book is on managing discipline and grievance within employment. It will be useful to devote a few lines to the meaning of the word 'employee'. It is probably best stated by Wallington (2007):

> Since the late nineteenth century, the cornerstone of the law relating to employment has been the contract of employment. This is so in relation not only to long-standing common law rights and obligations but also in relation to the modern statutory rights which can normally only be exercised by an 'employee'. Thus, a person whose employment has been terminated may be able to claim unfair dismissal or a redundancy payment, and a pregnant employee may be able to insist on returning to her employment after child-birth. The legislation gives such rights to employees, and then defines an employee quite simply as someone 'under a contract of employment' (which is not then further defined).

An employee is treated differently from a self-employed worker, independent contractor or agency staff (although this may change). Generally speaking an employee is someone who shares a mutuality of obligations with the employer and answers 'yes' to the following questions:

1. Does the worker undertake to provide their own time, work and skill in return for remuneration?
2. Is there a sufficient degree of control to enable the worker fairly to be called an employee?
3. Are there any other factors inconsistent with the existence of a contract of employment?

The distinction is important because, although health and safety and working time rules apply to all workers, discipline, rights to submit grievances, and incidentally employment tribunals, are concerned only with employees.

CHANGE AND CHANGE MANAGEMENT

It has been said that the only constant in industry and commerce is 'change'. The nature of work was subject to enormous change during the 18th, 19th and 20th centuries. For example, a great deal of manufacturing industry has migrated to developing countries and has been replaced by new sectors such as service industries and IT. Many workers have had to be retrained and 'socialized' into new working environments.

This has also had an impact on how discipline standards are set and enforced. There are examples of coal miners moving to small IT-based manufacturing, and workers from clothing factories moving to call centres or the service industry. Many organizations have a workforce with very different cultural backgrounds. In addition, migration has introduced workers with different origins, standards and expectations.

On the subject of change, it is now the fashion to embark on periodic change management programmes within many organizations. This process is sometimes accompanied by a structural reorganization and changes in management with new responsibilities. Revised reporting lines create confusion, and if not subject to careful planning, consultation and communications could present discipline problems. Structural and organizational change does often result in an increase in grievances.

THE NEW MANAGER

Discipline is sometimes a problem for the new manager. This is particularly so if their predecessor adopted a more relaxed or tolerant style. A newly appointed manager should be careful not to become drawn into accepting or condoning dubious practices, even if they have been commonplace, for example:

▪ initiation ceremonies with new recruits;
▪ falsification of timesheets in respect of work times and overtime;
▪ playing dangerous practical jokes;
▪ minor theft of goods or products.

Again, the manager would be well advised to issue a warning before launching into individual disciplinary action. Equally so, it would be wrong to take no action under the assumption that matters will improve. The longer these things are left the more difficult it becomes. Remember, the situation has the potential to reflect adversely on your capability as a manager. Case study 1 includes this possibility.

You are advised to study Chapter 2 on 'proactive discipline' carefully; this should be a good starting point in your efforts to create a disciplined environment if the one you inherit on transfer or promotion is less than satisfactory.

CHAPTER OUTLINES

This is not a book on employment law although the advice does reflect recent legislation and 'best practice'.

Chapter 1 deals with the dynamic legal framework including change to take effect during 2009, the policies and procedures within individual organizations and the guidance provided by the Advisory, Conciliation and Arbitration Service (ACAS). It sets out the practical skills, techniques and tactics necessary to support these sources in a manner that will be relevant to most situations.

Chapter 2 deals with the concept of _proactive discipline_. The word 'proactive' means 'tending to initiate change rather than reacting to events', and this is precisely what this chapter is about. Very few owners or managers relish dealing with discipline formally, and this chapter is about avoiding it wherever and whenever possible. Concepts such as management responsibilities, standard setting and, surprisingly, recruitment will be dealt with here. Use of the probation clause and induction are explained and good practice recommended.

By way of contrast, **Chapter 3** addresses _reactive discipline_, the skills and tactics necessary to take the right actions at the right time. The difference between internal and external complaints is dealt with. Managers need the skill to recognize that an apparently minor issue, like absenteeism or conduct outside work, has the potential to develop into a grievance or discipline investigation.

Chapter 4 deals with the subject of grievances, including whistleblowing, which can be the precursor to a discipline case although it often stands alone. Grievances can be seen by some as a potential source of aggravation and by others as a means of resolving employee concerns. While many of the skills necessary to investigate and resolve a grievance are the same as with discipline investigations, the subject requires separate treatment.

Chapter 5 is a brief but important look at issues relating to suspending employees from their duties pending discipline investigations. In addition, advice is given on the reintroduction of suspended staff to the workplace.

Although not normally a discipline issue, the concept of capability often gets confused with discipline and in many organizations it is regrettably contained in the same policy. For this reason and the fact that getting a capability dismissal wrong can lead to similar legal sanction, **Chapter 6** deals with this matter.

Discipline and grievance issues arise in a multitude of areas, and **Chapter 7** looks at these in some detail. Issues ranging from harassment and bullying to discrimination, and even drugs and alcohol are set in the context of discipline and grievances. An employer needs to ensure that staff are treated fairly and do not suffer any detriment or victimization as a result of being different in any way.

In order to reach a conclusion on whether an allegation is substantiated or not, an investigator needs to establish the facts. Evidence and evidence gathering are addressed in **Chapter 8.** This includes an examination of the burden and standard of proof required in discipline cases. In addition, we look at the increasingly difficult area of IT-related evidence and the misuse of IT. We introduce the concept of 'points to prove', which leads directly into the following three chapters.

In **Chapter 9** we take a look at investigation techniques and skills. This is a key element of the book and is necessarily based on the concepts already addressed. The investigator's skill set is designed to provide a wide range of tools for any investigator. While the detailed investigation of financial irregularities is outside the scope of this book, some advice and guidance is given on this complex area.

One special skill is at the core of any investigation, and this is interviewing. **Chapter 10** looks at this separately and in some detail. A variety of interviewing models are presented and set against a variety of situations and witness.

Logically, the next stage should be report writing and **Chapter 11** tackles this. The grading of findings and recommendations is the key to the decisions others must take. The making of extraneous recommendations is also addressed.

As far as the investigating officer is concerned, the disciplinary hearing is usually the end of the matter. **Chapter 12** looks at this from the perspective not only of the investigator but of the chair and others who may be involved in the disciplinary hearing. Appeals are a specific issue in both discipline and grievance cases, and we look at grounds of an appeal and how to deal with appeals. Any discipline and grievance can cause ripples in an organization. Dealing with the follow-up or aftermath needs to be part of the overall strategy, and we look at this.

Chapter 13 contains the case studies referred to throughout the book. **Chapter 14** contains a series of precedents and specimen documents.

1

Setting the structure

THE BASICS

The discipline and grievance procedures of any employer, no matter how small, are subject to specific legal requirements. An employer can agree to more complex and detailed arrangements; however, employers cannot contract to any procedure less robust than that basic or minimum procedure set out by law and Advisory, Conciliation and Arbitration Service (ACAS) codes. The contract of employment or written particulars of employment required by law (Employment Rights Act 1996 section 1(2)) must contain, among other matters, 'the disciplinary rules and procedures, and the name of a person to whom the employee can apply they are dissatisfied with any disciplinary action, or seeking redress of any grievance relating to her employment'(Employment Rights Act 1996 section 3(1)).

As an alternative the law does allow for these items to be contained in separate documents such as staff handbooks provided these are reasonably accessible and referred to in the main statement.

If your company does not conform to these minimum requirements, urgent action needs to be taken to ensure that its system is put right. You are strongly advised to set about drafting a set of policies relating to discipline and grievance. The ACAS website (www.acas.org.uk) is a good starting point.

If your organization has comprehensive discipline and grievance policies and procedures you may be tempted to pass on this section; I would ask you to resist this impulse. There are a variety of associated matters to bear in mind and there are also significant changes afoot during 2009 which I shall explain.

It is essential that any managers considering disciplinary action or who may be appointed as investigating officers should be fully conversant with their organization's policies and procedures, the relevant legislation and the relevant ACAS codes of practice.

STATUTORY DISPUTE RESOLUTION PROCEDURES

The standard dismissal and disciplinary procedures apply when an employer contemplates dismissing or taking relevant disciplinary action against an employee. They will remain in force until April 2009 at the earliest.

'Relevant disciplinary action' means action short of dismissal taken against the employee on account of conduct or capability, but does not include the giving of oral or written warnings. Relevant action could include (for example):

- demotion or downgrading, which would, however, only be lawful if the particular course of action was authorized in the employee's contract of employment as a disciplinary penalty;
- reallocation of duties following an ill-health absence;
- awarding a lower bonus than usual because of poor performance.

You are advised to follow your organizational policy in every case, even minor issues.

Although the focus of this book is the internal discipline and grievance process, it is important that managers know the basic procedures that might be followed in the event that their actions were scrutinized should a case end up in a claim.

As I write, employers are required to follow a *specific statutory minimum procedure* if they are contemplating dismissing an employee or imposing some other disciplinary penalty (see above) that is not suspension on full pay or a warning. If an employee is dismissed without the employer following this statutory procedure, and makes a claim to an employment tribunal, providing they have qualifying service of one continuous year (a continuous year is not necessary in discrimination, whistleblowing or a range of other matters) the dismissal will be automatically ruled unfair.

The statutory procedure is the current minimum requirement, and even where the relevant procedure is followed the dismissal may still be unfair if the employer has not acted reasonably in all the circumstances. What started as a relatively minor issue could escalate into a claim if it is not dealt with correctly.

In small organizations (and this is not specifically defined) it may not be practical to adopt all the detailed good practice guidance set out in ACAS codes of practice. Employment tribunals will take account of an employer's size and administrative resources when deciding whether it acted reasonably. However, all organizations regardless of size must follow the minimum statutory procedures. The procedures introduced in 2009 will be more 'friendly' to the small employer in an attempt to keep cases out of court and to reduce costs.

From a practical point of view, some managers in small firms may see the dismissal of an employee for poor attendance to be a simple matter. It might be something like 'warn them once then sack them next time'. I know from my work acting for claimants in Citizens Advice Bureaux and for respondents (employers) in private practice that this is not the case. Furthermore the lesson can be quite expensive. You must have and follow a fair and consistent procedure.

Standard statutory dismissal and disciplinary procedure (DDP)

This procedure applies to dismissal and disciplinary action short of dismissal based on either conduct or capability (although I strongly recommend a specific process in the area of capability / incompetence). It also applies to other dismissals such as expiry of a fixed-term contract, redundancy and retirement. In these areas, redundancy and retirement have their specific processes to be adhered to. The new Employment Bill will remove the non-renewal of a fixed-term contract and redundancy from the list of terminations required to follow a set procedure.

Step 1: statement of grounds for action and invitation to meeting

- The employer must set out in writing the employee's alleged conduct or characteristics which lead it to contemplate dismissing the employee or taking disciplinary action.
- The employer must send the statement or a copy of it to the employee and invite the employee to attend a meeting to discuss the matter.

Step 2: the meeting

▌ The meeting must take place before action is taken, except in the case where the disciplinary action consists of suspension.
▌ The meeting must not take place unless:
  – the employer has informed the employee what the basis was for including in the statement under Step 1 the ground or grounds given in it; and
  – the employee has had a reasonable opportunity to consider their response to that information.
▌ The employee must take all reasonable steps to attend the meeting.
▌ After the meeting, the employer must inform the employee of its decision and notify them of the right to appeal against the decision if they are not satisfied with it.
▌ Employees have the right to be accompanied at the meeting.

Step 3: appeal

▌ If the employee wishes to appeal, they must inform the employer.
▌ If the employee informs the employer of their wish to appeal, the employer must invite them to attend a further meeting.
▌ The employee must take all reasonable steps to attend the meeting.
▌ The appeal meeting need not take place before the dismissal or disciplinary action takes effect.
▌ Where reasonably practicable, the appeal should be dealt with by a more senior manager than attended the first meeting (unless the most senior manager attended that meeting).
▌ The employer must inform the employee of its final decision.
▌ Employees have the right to be accompanied at the appeal meeting.

If the employee refuses to attend the meeting and has no reasonable excuse, such as sickness, insufficient time to prepare or unavailability of the 'companion' (in which case it should be rearranged once), the matter should be heard in their absence.

Modified statutory dismissal and disciplinary procedure

Step 1: statement of grounds for action

▌ The employer must set out in writing:
  – the employee's alleged misconduct which has led to the dismissal;
  – the reasons for thinking at the time of the dismissal that the employee was guilty of the alleged misconduct;

– the employee's right of appeal against dismissal.
▌ The employer must send the statement or a copy of it to the employee.

Step 2: appeal

▌ If the employee does wish to appeal, they must inform the employer.
▌ If the employee informs the employer of a wish to appeal, the employer must invite them to attend a meeting.
▌ The employee must take all reasonable steps to attend the meeting.
▌ After the appeal meeting, the employer must inform the employee of its final decision.
▌ Where reasonably practicable the appeal should be dealt with by a more senior manager not involved in the earlier decision to dismiss.
▌ Employees have the right to be accompanied at the appeal meeting.

The Regulations state that the modified procedure may be used where the employee has committed an act of very serious misconduct and the circumstances are such that it is reasonable for the employer to dismiss the employee immediately without carrying out an investigation. The modified procedure requires only that the employer should write to the employee after the dismissal explaining the reason for the dismissal and allow them a right of appeal.

This procedure may be acceptable in small and medium business in the specific circumstances set out above. However, larger organizations, and in particular public sector bodies, may find that their policies do not allow use of the modified procedure. The alternative is to suspend the employer against whom the allegation is made, conduct an investigation, a discipline hearing, and if appropriate dismiss the person at the end of this process. It is good practice to use the standard procedure wherever possible.

ACAS CODE OF PRACTICE ON DISCIPLINARY AND GRIEVANCE PROCEDURES

The ACAS code of practice of October 2004 is the current version. This excellent document gives wide-ranging advice on dealing with discipline and grievances. Many of its principles are included in this book. If you are responsible for discipline or you may be called on to undertake an investigation, you must be aware of the code.

A failure to follow any part of the code, including the sections of an advisory nature, does not in itself make a person or organization liable to proceedings. In this respect the code is not law in itself. However, employment tribunals take the code into account. This means that if a discipline case does reach the stage of an employment tribunal claim, the conduct of the investigator and employer will come under scrutiny not only against the relevant law but against the advice in the ACAS code.

ORGANIZATIONAL POLICIES AND PROCEDURES

The law requires employers to have a discipline and grievance procedure. This, together with the ACAS code, is enough to ensure that their actions are steered along the correct path.

However, many organizations choose to draft a specific discipline and grievance policy relevant to their needs. This normally follows a process of consultation with trade unions and other consultative bodies. These policies establish a more complex process and explain the procedure in more detail, give guidance in areas such as suspension, investigation, hearings and appeals, and contain elements over and above the statutory minimum procedure. They may set out formats for the various letters to be used and the final disciplinary report. However, it is stressed that discipline procedures should be seen as a way of helping and encouraging employees rather than simply imposing sanctions.

My advice is that organizational policies should always be followed closely; failure to do so could result in internal challenges at a discipline hearing or give grounds for an appeal.

MISCONDUCT AND GROSS MISCONDUCT

Many discipline policies set out the types of behaviour that could be deemed to be *misconduct*, such as:

- absenteeism – particularly short-term and unpredictable;
- poor timekeeping;
- refusal to obey instructions: depending on the circumstances this could be seen as serious;
- administrative breaches: again the circumstances may make this a serious issue;
- breaches of standing operating procedures;
- minor health and safety breaches;

- minor breaches of IT rules, including misuse of e-mails and the internet.

Gross misconduct is misconduct so serious that so far as the contract of employment is concerned it entitles the employer to dismiss without notice. However, employers are strongly recommended to take more formal action through an investigation and discipline hearing. The terms 'gross' and 'serious' when used in combination with misconduct would seem to be interchangeable. The following list gives examples of offences that would be deemed to be gross misconduct. The list is not exhaustive:

- Theft, fraud, deliberate falsification of documents.
- Other offences of dishonesty.
- Falsification of a qualification that is a stated requirement of the employee's employment or results in financial gain to the employee.
- Falsification of records, reports, accounts, expense claims or self-certification forms whether or not for personal gain.
- Fighting or assault on another person, or other physical violence.
- Deliberate damage to or misuse of company property (or that belonging to clients, staff or visitors).
- Serious breach of trust and confidence,
- Discrimination, harassment or bullying of an individual, or group on the grounds of sex, sexual orientation, race, disability, age, or religious belief,
- Sexual misconduct at work.
- Being unfit for work through use of alcohol or illegal drugs.
- Possession, custody or control of illegal drugs on the company's premises.
- Serious or gross negligence.
- Undertaking unauthorized private work.
- Inappropriate behaviour: circumstances could render this to be mere misconduct.
- Serious insubordination.
- Unauthorized entry to files, records or computer records.
- Serious breach of the company's rules, including, but not restricted to, health and safety rules and rules on computer use.
- Serious breaches of IT rules, for example downloading inappropriate material.
- Serious breach of confidentiality.
- Conduct, actions or omissions that bring the company into disrepute.
- Conviction of a criminal offence that is relevant to the employee's employment (more on this later).

The ACAS code suggests that the procedures should follow natural justice in that the following should be in the policy:

▌ Before any discipline hearing employees are informed in advance of the allegations that are being made against them together with the supporting evidence, and employees are given the opportunity of challenging the allegations and evidence before decisions are reached.

▌ Employees should have the right of appeal against any decisions taken.

▌ The rules should be non-discriminatory.

▌ They should provide for matters to be dealt with quickly and within specified time limits.

▌ They should deal with the issue of confidentiality.

▌ They should specify the levels of management that have the authority to take various forms of disciplinary action.

▌ The rules should ensure that immediate supervisors do not normally have the power to dismiss without reference to senior management.

▌ The rules should ensure that, except for gross misconduct, no employee is dismissed for a first breach of discipline.

THE NEW PROVISIONS

Since their implementation in October 2004, the statutory dismissal and disciplinary procedures have been severely criticized for failing in their main purpose, which was to assist employers and employees in dealing with their disputes prior to reaching an employment tribunal. Following the Gibbons Review (Gibbons 2007) published in March 2007, the government reviewed the methods for resolving employment disputes. The basis intention was to simplify the current system, reduce costs to employers and employees and preserve existing rights. The three-step approach described above was thought to create expectations of a tribunal rather than a resolution, was excessive in its application to fixed-term contracts and appeals within small businesses, and in some cases, drove people towards legal advice with the associated costs.

The Employment Bill has been published, and among other issues, proposes to abolish the dismissal and grievance procedures. The commencement date is, at the time of going to press, spring 2009.

The Bill sets out to make changes to the law relating to dispute resolution in the workplace. It repeals the existing statutory procedures and related provisions about procedural unfairness in dismissal cases. ACAS will be publishing revised codes of practice on discipline and grievance, and employment tribunals will be able to adjust awards where parties have unreasonably failed to follow the code. In practical terms the changes will serve to repeal the current prescriptive three-step statutory procedures and provide clear, simple, non-prescriptive guidelines on grievances, discipline and dismissal.

The basic requirements will be:

▌ Employers and employees should do all they can to resolve disciplinary and grievance issues in the workplace. Recourse to an employment tribunal should only be a last resort.
▌ Issues should be dealt with promptly and consistently.
▌ Appropriate investigations should be made to establish the facts.
▌ Grievance and disciplinary meetings should be held by an independent manager if possible.
▌ Performance or capability issues should involve the immediate line manager.
▌ Employees should be informed of the basis of the problem and have an opportunity to put their case at a meeting.
▌ There should be a right to be accompanied.
▌ An appeal should be allowed to any formal decision.

It will be seen that there are significant changes in the period of direct interest to us in this book – that is before the claim is made. This is the critical period from the instigation of discipline, through the making of an allegation, the submission of a formal or informal grievance to any resolution, resignation or dismissal. This period offers the best opportunity to make a cost-effective impact on employer–employee relationships. In fact, the period from the start of employment offers an equally good opportunity to prevent discipline and grievance issues; see Chapter 2 on 'proactive discipline'.

ACAS will be also offering a new, free pre-claim resolution service to provide an option when internal resolution is struggling before an employer or employee enters a claim to an employment tribunal. In addition, the free ACAS telephone, and possibly e-mail, helpline will be expanded.

THE RIGHT TO BE ACCOMPANIED

The right to be accompanied is a legal entitlement in respect of discipline and grievance processes, but it is restricted. Any employee who is invited to attend a formal disciplinary interview (this is a confusing word as this really relates to the discipline hearing at which the employee could be subject to a sanction) or grievance hearing relating to contractual obliga-tions has the right (if they wish) to be accompanied by a 'companion'. The companion may be a fellow employee or a trade union official (this is an official employed by any trade union, who does not need to belong to a trade union recognized by the employer), or a lay trade union official, as long as they have been certified in writing by their union as having expe-rience of, or having received training in acting as an employee's compan-ion at disciplinary or grievance hearings. There is no statutory right for the employee to bring anyone else to the interview (for example a partner, spouse or solicitor).

The companion selected by the employee is under no legal obligation to accompany them to a disciplinary or grievance hearing. If, however, the chosen companion is another employee of the same organization and agrees to fulfil this role, they must be granted paid time off work to do so.

If an employee's chosen companion is unavailable to attend the hearing at the time nominated by the employer, the employee has the right to request a postponement of the hearing to a date within five working days of the original date. Such a postponement must be reasonable and may only be requested once.

Employers and managers in organizations that do not have trade union representation need to be aware that an employee in a discipline and most grievance processes has the right to ask for a companion. Failure to allow this statutory right could result in a claim and a finding of automatic unfair dismissal.

It is important to note that the right to be accompanied at disciplinary or grievance hearings extends not only to employees but also to 'workers' such as contract staff, home workers, casual or seasonal workers, agency temps and some freelancers, whatever the nature of the contractual rela-tionship. The right does not, however, apply to people who are genuinely self-employed. Investigations sometimes involve people who are not employees and this right should not be missed.

Disciplinary hearings, for these purposes, include meetings where either disciplinary actions or some other actions might be taken against the employee. Appeal hearings are also covered, as are any meetings held after an employee has left employment.

The companion can make representations at the hearing but cannot answer questions for the employee. The atmosphere of meetings at which 'companions' attend can be supportive and the business made more effec-tive for both sides by an experienced trade union official being present. Occasionally, however, an official's presence can make matters much more difficult. The investigator or discipline hearing chairperson needs to maintain control as far as is possible.

Informal discussions or counselling sessions do not attract the right to be accompanied unless they could result in formal warnings or other actions. It is important to note that meetings to investigate an issue are not 'disciplinary hearings' for the purpose of this right, unless of course the organizational policy allows accompaniment.

The right to be accompanied also applies to a hearing to resolve a grievance. For the purposes of this right, a grievance hearing is a meeting at which an employer deals with a complaint about a duty owed by it to an employee, whether the duty arises from statute or common law (for example contractual commitments such as a safe working environment and agreed working hours). For instance, an individual's request for a pay rise is unlikely to fall within the definition, unless a right to an increase is specifically provided for in the contract or the request raises an issue about equal pay. Equally, most employers are under no legal duty to provide their employees with car parking facilities, and a grievance about such facilities would carry no right to be accompanied at a hearing by a companion. However, if an employee were disabled and needed a car to get to and from work, this employee probably would be entitled to a companion at a grievance hearing, as an issue might arise of whether the employer was meeting its obligations under the Disability Discrimination Act 1995. The organizational policy may contain provisions to extend this legal right to all grievance hearings.

If employees are disabled, employers should consider whether it might be reasonable to allow them to be accompanied because of their disability. The same logic applies to young employees, vulnerable adults and employees who have a limited understanding of English.

In the same way that employers should cater for an employee's disability at a disciplinary or grievance hearing, they should also cater for a companion's disability, for example providing for wheelchair access if necessary.

The companion should be allowed to address the hearing in order to:

▌ put the employee's case;
▌ sum up the employee's case, or
▌ respond on the employee's behalf to any view expressed at the hearing.

The role is dealt within in more detail in Chapter 13.

THE SMALL EMPLOYER

Much of this detail might seem daunting to a small employer with a handful of staff. The duties of an employer are onerous and seem to be increasing year by year. It would be ideal for a small employer to have a full suite of policies and procedures but this is impractical for the small hairdresser, jobbing builder, publican, shopkeeper and so on. The absolute minimum a small employer is advised to have is:

▌ An offer letter detailing the key terms and conditions of the employ-ment and a written acceptance.

▌ A written contract or statement of terms and conditions, provided within two months and including such matters as:
  – date employment starts and end (if a fixed-term contract);
  – place of work, or extent of mobility;
  – brief outline of the job or job description;
  – pay and methods of calculating pay, plus frequency of pay;
  – hours of work;
  – holidays, plus public holidays;
  – rules relating to sickness, including injury;
  – notice required by either party to terminate contract;
  – details of pension provisions, usually access to a stakeholder scheme;
  – retirement age (an employer would need to justify a retirement age under 65);
  – discipline rules;
  – grievance rules.

▌ A proper induction process.

▌ Health and safety rules and procedures.

▌ Equal opportunities and diversity statements.

This list represents the bare minimum requirements. Certain business will require contractual clauses to protect business secrets whilst people are employed, and sometimes after their employment ends.

'INTERVIEW' AND 'HEARING'

One final point is the use of confusing terms. Individual pieces of legisla-tion, codes of practice and textbooks use these terms in different ways. For the purposes of this book I define them as follows:

▌ The **discipline interview** is when a manager or an investigator speaks to an employee about a disciplinary matter. It is not the stage at which the employee is at risk of any sanction. It is an opportunity for the employee, if they so choose, to put their side of the story or explain the reason for their actions or inaction. There is no legal right to be accom-panied at this stage although many organizational policies will grant this right and require the offer to be made.

- The term **disciplinary hearing** relates to the stage at which the evidence is heard, explanations are received and a decision is made. It is the stage at which the employee is at risk of a sanction, and in certain circumstances could be dismissed. There is a legal right to be accompanied at this stage. This includes an appeal.
- The **disciplinary officer** is the person who chairs the hearing, as opposed to the **investigator** who gathers and presents the evidence.

2

Proactive discipline

THE MEANING OF PROACTIVE

The dictionary definition of 'proactive' is 'taking the initiative by acting rather than reacting to events'. This is precisely the point of this chapter and of proactive discipline. Without doubt, this is potentially one of the most important concepts leading towards the prevention of discipline issues. The remainder of the book sets out techniques, tactics and procedures to assist you in dealing with grievances and discipline should the need arise. If you follow the advice contained in this chapter you will make a great deal of formal discipline, and probably grievances, unnecessary.

The ultimate aim is that all managers, directors, and even 'organizations' should develop the mindset of proactive discipline. The most productive environment is one of self-discipline in which colleagues internalize the concept of mutual respect, fairness, good discipline and adherence to rules and procedures. Quite simply, it is the setting out of rules and standards of behaviour that all your people feel part of, have contributed to and can see the sense of.

A second best is the creation of an environment in which individuals know the rules, the standards of behaviour expected of them and the key fact that the organization will not accept anything less. Idealistic and unachievable some might say. Maybe not! Proactive discipline is about striving towards these states. It is not about creating automatons but a work force in which initiative, team work and mutual respect can thrive. Discipline, like fairness, equality and safety, should be a subliminal thread throughout the organization.

POLICIES AND PROCEDURES

A good starting point is that of contractual requirements, policies, practices, protocols and 'standing operating procedures' (SOPs). These can be found in employment contracts, policy documents, staff handbooks, operations manuals and so on. Policies and procedures are necessary for:

- standardizing processes;
- securing fairness and consistency;
- ensuring the health and safety of staff and others;
- establishing and maintaining good relationship, especially towards minority groups;
- setting standards of behaviour;
- removing the need to 'reinvent the wheel' on a regular basis;
- learning from experience.

Chapter 1 considered discipline and grievance policies. Other examples include recruitment and selection, health and safety, sickness absence management, equality of opportunities and diversity, and whistleblowing. Large organizations have comprehensive sets of policies and procedures. Smaller firms sometimes have no policies at all, and discover the folly of this when contentious issues arise. It is sound advice to develop policies and procedures in key areas.

Having made this general point, I ought to mention the generic policy folder that is never opened, let alone circulated. Key policies should be available to _all_ members of staff, included in induction and other training programmes, and reviewed on a preset timetable and earlier when the law or situations change. They should be internally consistent and logical but also consistent with each other. It is not uncommon to find company policies and procedures, probably obtained from various sources, including the internet, which set out conflicting guidelines and procedures. This could be a recipe for confusion and a loophole for some to wriggle out of discipline allegations. Illogical policies and procedures also reflect the importance the organization places on its responsibilities in this regard. They will not be considered favourably if they are ever presented at an employment tribunal.

RECRUITMENT AND SELECTION

As organizations develop in size and complexity, the need to find the right people to carry out various tasks, roles and responsibilities becomes crucial. It is universally accepted that people make the 'real' difference in organizational performance. Therefore, the process of recruitment and selection emerges as an important function in itself. Managers should realize that this is equally the case whether recruitment is from outside the organization or via an internal promotion or transfer. Recruitment and selection of supervisors and managers is an especially important element in developing proactive discipline. While it is important that policies and legal requirements are followed, recruitment is too important to leave exclusively to the HR/personnel people. Even worse, it is not advisable to leave recruitment to an external agency without taking the trouble to conduct a robust selection process of the candidates presented to you using criteria important to the role in your organization. It is essential that line managers get involved at every stage of the process.

There is always an element of risk in recruitment from outside the organization. I mention the dangers of CV fraud later. The process you adopt needs to eliminate, as far as possible, the possibility of employing the wrong person. In personnel terms, your recruitment process must possess a good 'reliability factor'.

The consequences of getting recruitment wrong can be serious in discipline, team morale, customer relations, personal credibility, operational efficiency, time, and of course cost.

There are many facets to recruitment but it is important that you consider the impact the new employee or promoted member of staff is going to have on the organization. Simple job analysis is important because it provides the information on which to base two important types of document – the job description and the person specification. It is, of course, possible to carry out recruitment without job analysis but the likelihood that selection decisions will be properly objective and capable of identifying the most appropriate candidates for appointment is much reduced.

Any job can be categorized by what people need to know to be able to undertake the role, what they need to be able to do – the skills they need and *how they need to behave towards others*.

Knowledge can be technical or academic knowledge, processes and procedures, systems, markets, people etc. It can be established by academic or vocational qualifications, occupational testing or at an interview. Given a reasonable level of intelligence and aptitude, it can be developed and improved.

Skills can be technical skills, engineering, interpersonal, attention to detail, communication, writing, IT, physical, networking and so on. These can, and should, be assessed by a range of methods including testing and observation.

Behaviour can for example cover leadership, interpersonal skills, enthusiasm, assertiveness, team skills, sensitivity and creativity. These are more difficult to assess accurately but can make the difference between success and failure.

What is the difference between _behaviour_ and _attitude_? Obviously, a potential employer would like to be sure that an applicant possesses the desired range of attitudes suitable to the particular post and the organization in general. This is not as easy at it may seem. Attitudes are notoriously difficult to measure with any degree of reliability, and particularly so over the short period of a recruitment interview. Psychometric testing may help, as will good interviewing, but they are not foolproof.

People's attitudes are shown to the world by the way they behave. Human beings are very capable of behaving differently from the way they feel, particularly in the short term! An employer can only demand appropriate behaviour; hopefully attitudinal changes will follow.

Do not forget that recruitment is a two-way process. Not only are you looking at a range of candidates to decide whether they are suitable for your organization, they are looking at you to decide whether you and your colleagues represent an organization they wish to work for. If they are not doing this, do you really want them?

It is essential that the interview process asks candidates about their attitude to discipline, probes their experiences in this area and tries to imagine how they will fit in with those already in position. _Always check references and qualifications_ and never take a risk in an appointment! If the right candidate does not present themself, particularly for a key role, review your advertising tactics, job / person specification and try again. If there is a doubt in anyone's mind there will be a reason for it. Remember, with a bright candidate you can develop their skills and knowledge, but you are unlikely to be able to change a person's attitude. _If the doubt is about a candidate's attitude towards others – do not appoint._ Failure to follow this advice can have a serious impact on your organization, its people, and can be costly. It can and does present itself in discipline, capability and / or sickness problems later.

Similar consideration should be applied to internal promotions. Taking on the role of supervisor or manager is not as easy as some imagine. Leadership is largely an inherent skill and some just do not have it in sufficient quantity or quality. It is not always a good plan to promote the most successful sales person to sales manager or appoint the best mechanic to workshop manager, unless of course they demonstrate the different range of skills, knowledge and attitudes necessary for the new role. Having made this point, internal promotions and appointments can reduce the risk in recruitment as you do know their background and work ethic.

CONTRACTS AND JOB DESCRIPTIONS

When you have made an appointment, particularly at supervisory or management level, ensure that the contract of employment, offer letter or statement of terms includes the responsibilities: for example, to work as part of a team, liase with others, supervise and/or manage others. If relevant, include the requirement to appraise or review others and take part in an appraisal or review process.

Include clauses in the contract of employment or statement such as:

▌ **Company policies.** You will be required to conform to the policies, procedures, rules and practices of 'The Company' as set out in this statement, offer letter, contract or staff handbook. Any changes to the policies, procedures, rules and practices will be communicated to you.

▌ **Amendment of terms.** Any alteration to these main particulars of employment will be discussed with you and recorded within one month of such alteration in all copies of the document referred to in this Statement. An up-to-date version of these documents will be held for inspection by [a Director and in the main office].

Every employee continuing in employment with 'The Company' for more than fourteen (14) days following either the issue of, or additions to, this Statement shall be deemed to have contracted with the company on the terms of the new or amended conditions.

You should specify in a job description what areas people are responsible for, and if appropriate, the teams people are required to manage. Spell out the requirement to comply with company policies is areas such as equality and diversity, and health and safety. Take steps to remove the potential defence of 'I didn't know it was my responsibility.' If you get the right people in place proactive discipline becomes much easier.

INDUCTION

Many organizations that do take care to recruit the right people fail to 'seal the bargain' by carrying out an effective induction programme. This is the process that really 'kick-starts' proactive discipline. It should raise questions such as:

▌ Does the job match the recruit's expectations or promises made to them?
▌ Can the new recruit deliver all that is expected formally and informally?
▌ Does the newcomer know where to get help, support or guidance?
▌ Is the new recruit aware of the key policies and procedures?
▌ Does the recruit really understand the culture of discipline?

Do you leave too much to line managers who are not skilled in training or personnel issues and who have many other priorities and demands on their time? Good induction procedures can ease the pressure on recruits and take them through the difficult times when they are considering whether they are in the right job or not. Effective induction is not a soft option, it is a 'best practice' linking directly into the achievement of business objectives and proactive discipline.

Stage 1 induction

This is the normal 'administrative' induction including matters such as sickness procedure, annual holidays, payments, health and safety, welfare matters, toilets, where to park your car and where not to park your car and so on. This is often a fast-moving procedure that takes in the geography of the premises, product or service knowledge, customer base and a succession of new faces and new names.

Do not forget to include the values of the organization, as set out in key policies regarding equality and diversity, including statements about discrimination, harassment and bullying. The secret is to take things slowly over a period of days. An overload of information only means it has to be given again. Reinforce the process with handouts and documentation for later reference, and in particular an organization chart.

Learning the hard way is not the only way of learning and it does produce too many casualties. It may have happened to you but that is no excuse to 'drop someone in at the deep end'. Statements like 'I had to learn the hard way, why shouldn't they?' are not helpful, but you still hear them expressed!

Remember to deal with all the key policies, procedures and rules. Ensure that they are listed on a checklist. Ensure that new employees tick and sign each item to acknowledge that they have been informed of and understand them. This can then be placed in their personal files and forgotten about – unless, of course, you need it in disciplinary action later! This document, when signed by the employee, overcomes the defence in many cases of failure to follow rules of 'I didn't know', or 'Nobody told me.'

Stage 2 induction

This stage relates to the hidden aspects of the business and is often not given to new recruits. This stage introduces newcomers to standards and expectations, team relationships, where to go for help, relationships with other sections of the business, flows of work, peaks and troughs, training and attendance requirements and so on. It should include formal and informal channels of communication. Perhaps someone could even mention any personal career opportunities available within the organization.

The induction process is not merely to complete a checklist (although this is important), it is to ease people into your organization, to make them feel that they have been chosen well, to develop their confidence, and crucially, to make the best of the time and money spent on recruitment.

The better organizations have detailed policy and procedures relating to induction in which the two stages are clearly identified. These often take the form of a structured training course held from time to time and usually include a visit by a senior member of staff.

Of course, many readers will be thinking this is all too formal for a company as small as theirs. I would counsel against this. Induction is important no matter how small the business, even a corner shop! Do not forget to draft the checklists for the recruit to sign at the end of the induction process.

PROBATION

Yet another tool in the proactive discipline armoury is probation. Every contract of employment or statement of terms of employment should contain a probation clause to cover the first three or six months of a new employee's service. The wording of the clause should be something like:

Probationary period

This appointment is subject to a probationary period of three/six months, during which time your performance will be reviewed. Subject to your assessment during your probationary period, your employment could be terminated, your probationary period extended to a maximum of [six] months or permanent employment confirmed.

If your employment is terminated under this provision, 'The Company' will give one week's notice or payment in lieu thereof.

Any termination of the probationary period shall not be seen as forming any part of the company's discipline procedure.

(Probationary period is not applicable to current employees)

A probation clause – a trial period – is recognized as best practice, and most employers will use the facility in their contracts. However, although the facility usually exists, the spirit of the process is not always followed correctly and it is often ignored altogether. It is not unusual to find organizations that have a probation policy but take no action unless it becomes clear that a recruit is patently unsuitable and urgent action needs to be taken.

A more proactive approach produces better results. Line managers should be required to report on the new recruit, at whatever level. This should take the form of a meeting and a report, for example in respect of a sixth-month period, on the first, third and fifth month. These reports assist staff to identify areas that need to be addressed at a time early enough to do something positive about them, and of equal importance, encourage line managers to discuss progress with the new member of their team. The recruit's attitude towards discipline is, of course, an area that should be included in the review.

At the end of the process a final report is required to formally acknowledge the fact that the probation period has been completed successfully. The final interview should take the form of a formal letter and a meeting with a senior member of staff.

If progress is not satisfactory action *must* be taken to inform the employee and clearly set out the standard required, monitor improvement, maybe extend the probation period or carry out a dismissal.

Employment protection rights against unfair dismissal are gained after only 12 months continuous service (Employment Rights Act 1966 Section 108(1)). After this dismissal becomes more problematic and carries a real risk of litigation. Dismissal on the grounds of capability (see Chapter 6) is an option at any stage but is a much more complex process, carrying some element of risk.

It is worth repeating that it may be possible to improve an employee's skill level and knowledge, particularly in areas they did not claim to have experience of on recruitment. It should be accepted as a presumption that you cannot improve a bad attitude or unacceptable interpersonal skills. *Do not take the risk!* If you have serious doubts use the probation clause while it is still in force and let someone else have the 'problem employee'.

There are three other points to make while discussing probation:

▌ It may only be that a new employee does not 'fit' in your organization. It does not always mean they are unemployable. If you carry out the probation assessment correctly and decide to ignore any warning signs, you do at least do it with full knowledge of the risks.

▌ Do not assume that probation is a process only for the lower grades. It is just as relevant for senior staff. My experience is that organizations that fail to exercise a probation dismissal after clear indications that a senor manager is unsuitable very often end up with heavy termination payments and considerable organizational disruption. Unfortunately, some senior managers or board members feel that a dismissal under a probation clause is tantamount to an admission that they made a mistake in the initial appointment. I have been involved in terminations in the NHS, education and central government that fall into this category and have ultimately cost the taxpayer six-figure sums.

▌ Do not assume that managers are competent and confident enough to carry out probation-type reviews without the necessary training. The competences associated with this area of work are not easy and many managers will require support to be effective. If your organization does have an appraisal or review process the training for these can be combined with that for probation-related reviews. (One of our case studies looks at the potential problems in using untrained interviewers.)

INFORMAL DISCIPLINE AND SETTING STANDARDS

The next stage in creating the proactive discipline environment is the exercising of informal discipline and the setting of standards, particularly relating to behaviour. Organizational discipline is undermined by the maxim 'Do as I say, not as I do!' Supervisors and managers must demonstrate self-discipline and appropriate behaviour towards others. Bullying and discriminatory behaviour should not be acceptable at any level. Staff should be treated fairly, reasonably and consistently. The point has been made that, in practical terms, the context of heavy industry is different from that of an accountancy office. Nevertheless, clear standards need to be set and adhered to. Bullying, harassment and discriminating are not acceptable anywhere.

Many serious discipline situations arise out of the fact that an organization or a particular manager failed to deal with minor infringements of rules. For example: .

▌ Failure to comment on minor tardiness can lead some to take advantage and report late frequently.
▌ Failure to deal with inappropriate language or racists/sexist jokes can create an environment for serious harassment or discrimination (remember the employer can be held vicariously liable for such actions).
▌ Failure to monitor the behaviour of 'strong characters' can lead to bullying which, among other things, can manifest itself in increased sickness, poor staff retention and low morale.
▌ Failure to question poor attendance, especially frequent and unpredictable single days sick, will lead to problems later.
▌ Failure to comment on excessive use of the firm's telephone for private calls can also lead to escalation of the problem.

There could be many more examples but the point to be made is that the sensitive yet regular exercise of informal discipline is the key to creating the right environment.

Some managers see very little past the technical elements of their job and the production or budgetary targets. When disciplinary issues arise they come as a surprise and can require formal action. To this end it may be necessary to provide managers and supervisors with training in their responsibilities with regard to discipline and grievances. This element of a manager's job should also be included as one of the assessment criteria in an appraisal scheme.

Taking early action, giving words of advice, issuing warnings about future conduct and challenging inappropriate behaviour are all tools available to the good manager to enforce informal discipline. Delivered in the correct way they should be seen as normal and helpful.

The public 'telling off' or 'rollicking' is not recommended. It is demeaning, demonstrates the type of bullying behaviour managers should seek to remove, not encourage, and often has the contrary effect to that intended. As opposed to praise, which is effective if given openly, discipline, formal or informal, should be carried out in private. Challenging someone's actions or behaviour is most effective when accompanied by a specific explanation of both the issues causing concern and the standard required in future. Managers should take time to ensure that their team understand what is required, the reasons for this requirement and the likely consequences if they continue with any unacceptable behaviour.

Where people work together there is always the potential for the development of close relationships or, indeed, conflict. Managers at all levels need to be aware of this, and while positive action is not always necessary, the situation should be monitored. In addition, managers should be aware of other issues affecting their staff, particularly looking out for indicators such as a changes in behaviour, issues of work quality or increased absenteeism. All these indicators, if not picked up and where appropriate addressed, can manifest themselves in discipline problems. Some of the more serious outcomes could be:

- absenteeism resulting from harassment or bullying;
- theft from the workplace or from colleagues because of drug dependency;
- quality of work issues resulting from personal problems at home or at work.

Managers may not have the skills to deal with this type of issue but they are unlikely to obtain the right assistance if they do not notice the signs; they are usually best placed to do so.

MANAGEMENT TRAINING

This seems a convenient place at which to briefly mention training of managers and supervisors. Employers will be aware that this costs money and time. However, I think it is essential that employers give some level of training to their managers, as an absolute necessity in areas such as:

- recruitment and selection, including interviewing and equality of opportunities;
- dealing with discipline and grievances, including simple investigations, diversity, discrimination, harassment and bullying;
- dealing with induction, probation and appraisal/reviews;
- absence management (start by using the term 'absence' as opposed to 'sick leave', which suggests an entitlement!).

The training need not be expensive and it is a good idea to use the organization's policies in that particular area as a framework for the training. There are a great many providers of training and some are very expensive. Larger organizations will, of course, have their own training and development sections. For those on a smaller budget, cost-effective training may be available via local chambers of commerce, ACAS and employers' associations. If budgets are tight, it is a good idea to trawl the personal files of staff to check who may have training experience in their work experience; they may be willing to assist in this area.

I strongly recommend that you give some level of training to managers in these areas. As a final point of encouragement, it is very common for employment judges to ask for company policies and details of the training given to managers and supervisors in the area subject of any claim. You can only imagine the impact of having to admit that you had neither policies nor training at the time.

THE 'LAST STRAW'

One particular phenomenon to bring to your attention while dealing with proactive discipline is the concept of the 'last straw'. If supervisors or managers do not buy in to the philosophy of proactive discipline they are left with the option of ignoring minor infringements or using the heavy stick of formal discipline unnecessarily and inappropriately. It must be stressed that the main intention of this book is to assist managers to avoid employment tribunals, and if possible formal discipline, but when it is necessary to deal with it correctly and effectively, thus mitigating, as far as is possible, the problems associated with employment litigation.

If managers do not deal with minor issues by way of informal discipline, some individuals will let their standards drop and take advantage. It is not uncommon for the first disciplinary action to be a formal interview. In many cases an early intervention can avoid this.

Do not permit matters to deteriorate to the level at which your patience finally gives way and you respond to an issue of minor discipline that does not warrant formal action. Do not let discipline matters pass without comment; be proactive!

DIFFICULT CONVERSATIONS

Dealing with the difficult conversation is a challenge to many supervisors and managers. The skills are relevant to formal discipline investigations but probably more so when seeking to enforce proactive discipline. Managers can find themselves holding a conversation about a wide range of difficult and sensitive issues including absenteeism, harassment, attitudes, attendance, personal hygiene (a particularly difficult area), inappropriate relations and bullying. They are stressful for even the most experienced manager whether the person with whom you are having the conversation is a victim or possible cause of the problem.

There are a couple of options available to a manager to avoid these confrontations. The first is to ignore the problem altogether, bury your head in the sand and hope it goes away. It will not go away and may be even more serious when it next confronts you. The employee involved may even raise the issue with a more senior manager and add the complaint that you did not deal with it. The second option is to direct the problem to human resources or personnel, and this is an option many managers take.

Effective management includes dealing with these issues, and while HR will assist and advise, the responsibility clearly rests with the line manager or supervisor. Think how your failure to act will impact on your reputation within your team and within the organization in general. You must tackle the issue yourself, but how?

There may be guidance in your policies and procedures and some may have had the benefit of training to fall back on. However, it will never be easy.

- You must deal with the issue as soon as possible. However, you should balance this with choosing an appropriate time and place, gaining a little background, if possible, and preparing for the meeting. You may not be able to plan how a difficult conversation will progress but you should decide how you intend to open the meeting. You should also consider what you would wish to achieve from the conversation, and also the minimum you would be prepared to accept.
- Of course, there will be times when planning is impossible, such as a serious disturbance within your team, maybe even a fight or when a distraught person enters your office.
- In extreme circumstances, and bearing in mind your policies, it may be advisable to send someone home for the rest of the day. In any event you should try to remove a 'victim' from the source of the complaint.
- When you do meet, consider whether it would be appropriate for you to be accompanied, or indeed whether your team member should be offered the chance of being accompanied. This will not be necessary in many cases.
- The way the meeting progresses will depend on the circumstances and whether you are holding a conversation with a 'victim' or someone who demonstrates behaviour you are seeking to correct.
- A victim should be reassured, put at ease and listened to; do not make assumptions. Regular pauses to summarize and rephrase the story are essential. Avoid writing notes at the beginning of a difficult conversation. Many of the skills associated with this are dealt with in detail in Chapter 10, about interviewing.

▌ If the person you are speaking to is not a 'victim' a slightly different approach may be called for. At this stage, I am assuming you are trying to deal with a difficult issue on an informal basis. It is a good tactic to confront the person with the facts if you know them. Remember, if you do have a criticism, such as an inappropriate attitude, unacceptable behaviour or personal hygiene, it is the behaviour you are concerned with, not that particular person. In some cases that person may not be aware of what they are doing or of the effect it has on others. Most people are concerned about the affect they have on their colleagues. Some people do not know how they come across to others. Do you?

▌ When you do ask questions remember to leave 'space' for the person to reply. Do not suggest a range of possible answers, such as 'Was it... or was it...?' Keeping appropriate eye contact, nodding and making encouraging sounds, can assist communication. Try to ensure that the balance of speaking is firmly on the side of the person you are holding the conversation with.

▌ Ask the person to consider the effect their behaviour is having on others. Ask for a commitment to change the offending behaviour. You should add that you, the team and the organization require such a change and the position will be monitored in the future. Be assertive yet calm.

▌ Keeping a diary note is optional but recommended in cases where you feel the problem may return.

There are many situations in which a difficult conversation may become necessary. If these situations are likely to result in a grievance or disciplinary action, or both, you must be careful to follow the correct procedures.

From time to time managers are required to tell team members they are at the risk of redundancy, a fixed-term contract is not being renewed, their probation period has not been successfully completed, the firm is relocating and so on. Similar tactics to those described above should be useful, but be careful not to make promises or assurances you are not in a position to deliver.

CONCLUDING COMMENTS

This chapter has dealt with a range of tactics to support the philosophy of proactive discipline. I commend the concept to you as an employer or manager. The benefits are many and the risks few. It is the keystone in any strategy to create and maintain a disciplined workplace. Treat people with respect, set standards, and enforce them by behaviour and action.

A great deal of the work covered by this book can be avoided by managers managing. This includes setting reasonable standards, developing an empathy with their team colleagues and not creating a situation in which there is one law for some and one for the rest. I know from my work in dealing with claimants that a great many problems are caused by managers being more concerned with their future than the present, and being more concerned with their next recruitment than their last one.

All this may seem a little dramatic but the rewards to be obtained from adopting a proactive discipline approach are real. However, people do raise grievances and they do break disciplinary rules. In addition, some people will simply not buy in to the concept of a disciplined environment, they see work as an opportunity to get one over the boss. These people need to be dealt with, and the following pages should tell you how.

3

Reactive discipline

If your efforts to create an atmosphere of proactive discipline are not yet fully embedded, there may be a need to 'react' to any discipline issues that may arise. If the issues are ones of performance you may also want to review Chapter 6 dealing with capability and the borderline decision when incompetence and misconduct are difficult to separate. Generally speaking these are separated by the fact that ill discipline requires a conscious intention to carry out some act or fail to take some action. Discipline is normally not an unconscious act, unless we categorize negligence and carelessness as such. In fact this type of behaviour often demonstrates a desire to push the barriers and boundaries of the organization in general, and its managers or supervisors in particular. The more a manager allows this to happen, the more difficult it becomes to impose any degree of discipline when matters begin to go wrong. That is not to say that discipline is at the forefront of a manager's mind – clearly that should be their role in the business, and the quality of their contribution to the core of the organization, be it production, service, education or social. When discipline begins to have an impact on this core role, action must be taken quickly.

THE PHILOSOPHY

The induction process should have been completed, the checklists explained and signed and the probation period successfully concluded. Through proactive discipline, line managers must ensure that employees are made aware of their responsibilities and the standards of conduct that are required (through induction training, feedback during one-to-one meetings and training in the organization's policies and procedures). A manager must demonstrate the required standards of behaviour by their own actions. If so the basic steps are in place.

The whole philosophy of discipline within an organization is usually set out in the preamble to the policy itself or management guidelines. The box below sets out statements that could be used in a discipline policy introduction and give examples of their impact.

Every effort will be made to avoid the use of disciplinary action where alternatives are appropriate.

Obviously a casual word or even a serious verbal warning are far preferable to disciplinary action. If the problem is one of conflict between employees, a face-to-face meeting could be helpful in some circumstances – in others less so.

The aim of this policy is to provide a framework for dealing with disciplinary issues on a fair and consistent basis and to encourage improvement in an employee whose conduct is below acceptable standards.

While different managers will always adopt different styles and set different standards of behaviour, a consistent approach is generally required throughout an organization. I mentioned the problems facing a new manager in the Introduction, and while a poor standard should not be acceptable, employees will need to be taken through the changes with a degree of understanding and sensitivity. If employees have been used to a less effective manager you should not expect a complete change within days, or possibly even weeks.

The policy should aid the effective management of people and should not be viewed primarily as a means of imposing sanctions or as leading to dismissal.

It should be clear to everyone that the discipline structure is aimed at achieving good standards of discipline and behaviour towards each other. Sanctions, including the ultimate deterrent of dismissal, are used to reinforce acceptable standards and only as a last resort. If you threaten discipline next time and the next time comes, take action. You can always draw back later if the circumstances warrant it. Maybe you should not commit yourself with a specific threat to take action next time. However, if you fail to follow up a threat with action you are placing yourself in a difficult position. It is important that line managers take early action. This features regularly in our credo of proactive discipline. Early actions can avoid formal discipline. 'I'm too busy to bother with minor issues.' 'The team will sort his behaviour out, I don't need to worry.' 'They are working well, why should I upset things by moaning about bad language and dirty jokes?' 'This is a busy workshop; they have to learn to accept the banter.' You will have heard similar statements and I could list dozens more. In simple terms, they are not acceptable.

Individuals have a contractual responsibility to carry out their duties to the best of their ability and to behave in a reasonable and professional manner, and should be given every help and encouragement to do so.

This is correct. However, the manager must be sure that their staff know this and understand the implications if they do not perform satisfactorily.

The line manager will discuss any issues in relation to an employee's conduct or behaviour as soon as these arise and will deal with the situation as a line manager in a reasonable and competent manner.

As an employer or senior manager, are you sure that your junior managers and supervisors have the necessary skills to deal with discipline reasonably and competently? If not, the results could be expensive. What are you going to do about it?

Where the required standards of conduct or behaviour are not achieved, disciplinary action will be taken.

This should be implicit in the policy and reinforced by the conduct of managers and the organization. Yes, there are steps there to be taken before formal discipline is brought into play, but employees must know that the process will be followed through when the situation demands it. Managers must not fail to carry out their duties and follow through with discipline if other tactics fail.

Obviously situations that arise under the general heading of discipline are not always clear-cut. For example in Case study 1 (see page 175), the matter seems relatively straightforward. The manager has been warned that his attitude towards minor discipline is not as the company would wish it to be. A discipline manner arises, he takes informal action, there is a repeat and he takes formal action to report the matter to a higher authority in accordance with the policy. This is relatively simple. However, consider what your reaction might be if the reply when you point out the facts and the evidence is something like:

As you know I have just moved in with my girlfriend. I have not told anyone but she has a disabled five-year-old child who needs to be taken to her day care unit every morning. My partner cannot drive and sometimes the taxi does not arrive on time, then I have to drop the child off. This makes me late.

Obviously, this puts an entirely different perspective on the situation. Of course, it might not be true, but let us assume that it is. Discipline would seem to be the wrong tool to deal with what seems to be a welfare problem. Family-friendly legislation even provides a right to ask for a variation of contract, possibly a change of starting times, in these circumstances.

It is a simple step to move from a discipline situation to a welfare problem. It is less so to move in the opposite direction, to move from treating a matter as a welfare problem or trivially to take formal discipline.

Another example of the same problem is when an employee is subject to discipline for not following detailed standard operating procedures, only to reveal later that they suffer from dyslexia or reading difficulties. It is not uncommon for employees to take sophisticated steps to hide this type of problem.

Discipline situations do not always end up the way they start. For example, short-term, unpredictable sickness is a problem for many organizations. In the case of a chronic illness or a recurring complaint, sickness procedures need to be followed, but in some cases the manager might suspect a degree of malingering. Discipline is often resorted to when persuasion and encouragement to improve attendance fails.

It sometimes turns out that attendance problems arise in situations of bullying or racial/sexual harassment. Again, it is easier to move from a formal discipline process to a welfare support role than in the opposite direction. Once you are in 'welfare mode', finding out you are wrong makes discipline problematic. Maybe this is thinking the worst of people and not giving them the benefit of any doubt. Obviously an employer or manager knows particular traits of their team. Any action totally out of character needs to be recognized and scrutinized carefully. There could be several reasons for a change in behaviour, such as:

- illness, including stress and illnesses at home;
- relationship problems, including in an employee's private life such as divorce;
- harassment or bullying;
- debt problems;
- carer responsibilities at home;
- changes in work patterns;
- changes in schedules, increased pressure and so on;
- changes in techniques, perhaps as a result of computerization.

The philosophy is therefore simple:

- Set clear standards of behaviour and performance.
- Be aware of the behaviour and performance of your team and the individuals within it.

■ Recognize changes in behaviour and/or performance.

■ React to minor breaches of discipline as and when they occur.

■ Deal with more frequent and serious breaches in accordance with the techniques explained in this book.

■ Be prepared to draw back from discipline if this seems the correct action to take.

REACTING TO MISCONDUCT

The way managers react to minor breaches of discipline is often symptomatic of their whole attitude towards discipline. Can minor issues be ignored? Let me explain this by giving a few examples.

Example 1

A team member takes a few single days off over a three- or four-week period. This is no big deal, or is it? Did you notice? You should have done, and you should have spoken to them after each day off. Say something like 'I noticed you were off yesterday, is everything OK?' 'Are you better now?' or 'This is the second/third day off this month, I was wondering if you were feeling well?' Of course, many larger organizations have a complex absence management policy, and 'return to work' interviews are part of it. Incidentally, it is generally agreed that short 'return to work' interactions at the immediate line manager level have a real and measurable impact on short-term unpredictable absence without the need to progress to heavier action.

Example 2

You are in your general office when you hear a male member of your team address a female colleague. 'I say, Jean, if that skirt was any shorter you'd be showing your knickers.' The woman smiles but seems mildly embarrassed. The man and woman always get along well and are of a similar age. There is no history of any friction. The woman makes no complaint to you and no one else in the office seems to be taking any notice. Is this an incident to ignore?

Very definitely not! You should choose an appropriate moment to tell the male employer that this type of comment is totally unacceptable and will not be tolerated. Responses like, 'She doesn't mind, she gives as good as she gets,' should not be accepted. The man should be left in no doubt that a repeat will be dealt with as a disciplinary matter. You may wish to speak to the woman, even though she did not complain, to reassure her that you do not accept this type of banter and have dealt with the situation. Believe me, your actions will be appreciated. Furthermore, a failure to take action could result in the employer and you, as a manager, facing a claim. A brief diary note would suffice. The matter should not be referred to again, unless, of course, there is a repeat.

Example 3

You are the manager and overhear a member of your team on the telephone. From the tone of the conversation and the one side you can hear, she is obviously dealing with a complaint or dissatisfied customer. You hear her say, 'I'm doing my best; if you're not satisfied you can take your bloody order somewhere else.' She then slams the telephone down. You do get difficult customers from time to time and they can be abusive.

Do you ignore this? No, it must be dealt with sensitively but it must be addressed. What did the customer say to provoke the reaction from your employee? You must speak to your employee in private and deal with the matter on its merits. However, your team must know that this type of behaviour is unacceptable and will be addressed.

Example 4

Some minor breaches will test your skills. For example, you enter the office to find John playing a computer game on his terminal. When you speak to him he says, 'Well, Joan and Peter have gone outside for a cigarette. Why should I have to work just because I don't smoke?' Alternatively, the reply could be, 'The mainframe has gone down again and I can't get into my files.'

The context of the office will have a bearing on the tactics you use, and of course, John has a point with regard to the smoking. The main outcome is that you recognize what is going on and respond to it.

Example 5

A member of the delivery team informs you that several packages of books sent by your unit burst open in the van, and that they were not in bubble-wrap in accordance with standard practice. This resulted in the books having to be repackaged and failing to meet the delivery deadline set by your firm's quality standards. When you look into this your section leader tells you that it was Friday afternoon, his team had several packages to get out and had run out of bubble-wrap. There was no time that afternoon to send someone to the stores for more.

This is bordering on serious misconduct, particularly as a supervisor seems to be the instigator. Has it happened before? This may be a case in which you feel you need to take formal disciplinary action. However, if the performance of the supervisory and team has been good you may wish to deal with it informally. There are two points to make:

▌ You cannot and should not ignore this type of issue.
▌ You cannot give a verbal warning ('a rollicking') and take disciplinary action at the same time.

If you decide on informal action it must be made clear to everyone that quality standards are critical to the continuing success of the company and failing to meet them is not acceptable. It might be advisable to follow this up with some spot checks over the next few weeks.

REACTING TO GROSS MISCONDUCT

As you will recall from our look at discipline policies, gross misconduct is the most serious form of misconduct. In fact, it is so serious that an employer is contractually entitled to dismiss the offender without notice. For serious offences like assault, theft, being under influence of drink or drugs, or serious insubordination, a small or medium employer may safely decide to summarily dismiss an employer. However, the dismissed employee may still have a claim for unfair dismissal (Employment Rights Act 1996, Section 230 (2)), as long as they have one year's continuous service.

Before taking this step a manager or employer should consider the context of the offence, its gravity and whether or not there may be mitigating circumstances. For example, an assault committed by a normally quiet employee may be as a result of intense harassment or bullying, or personal issues. While these are serious issues and cannot be justified, it is often better to take a more measured approach. In most cases the best method is to suspend those involved and conduct an investigation; this process will be outlined later.

There is a difference between a measured consideration of the circumstances followed by incisive action and a 'knee-jerk' reaction to summarily dismiss.

Chapters 8, 9 and 10 on evidence gathering, investigations and interviewing set out the procedures to follow in dealing with gross misconduct in some detail. However, even more than with minor breaches of discipline, serious breaches must be dealt with quickly and effectively.

It is fact that some gross misconduct is straightforward and requires little in the way of investigation. However, I would recommend that even if an employee is caught 'red-handed' committing an offence of gross misconduct such as theft, fighting and so on, it is still not sensible to dismiss on the spot. There may be a reason, justification, medical issues or mitigation that, while it may not change the decision, needs to be heard. It is better, and safer, to suspend and investigate followed by a standard procedure, including the opportunity of an appeal.

FORMAL ACTION OR NOT?

Some organizations will have clear procedural guidance dictating what a manager should do in specific situations and others may not. These questions may help in deciding what to do in the event of a disciplinary issue:

- Does my action have the potential to resolve the issue permanently?
- Will any complainant or customer accept the action I propose to take, formal or informal?
- Will my action reflect well on me as a manager?
- Will my actions have a positive impact on the work team?
- Am I acting within the policy and procedures of my employer?
- Will my actions be accepted by the employee committing the breach of contract?
- Am I sure the employee committing the breach of contract will not think they are 'getting away with it'?

If you answer 'yes' to all of these questions, go ahead. If there is a 'no', reconsider your decision. At the end of this process, take decisive action, and do not forget to reflect on and learn from the whole process.

CONDUCT THAT OCCURS OUTSIDE WORK

It is difficult to conceive of any conduct outside the employment not amounting to criminal behaviour or breaches of contract that could be used as the basis of any action by an employer other than in very specific circumstances. For example, consider a secondary school teacher leaving his spouse or partner and setting upon home with a 17-year-old. If this person is not a pupil there would be no crime but it may be considered unacceptable. Or consider a support worker in a multi-racial help centre joining the British National Party: again not criminal but it could be considered inappropriate.

I recall an incident involving British football supporters attending a European match in Marseilles some years ago. There was some serious disorder among the fans and several British men were arrested. This included some men who later turned out to be postmen. The prime minister at the time made a public comment to the effect that their employer should look at their behaviour and consider their continuing employment. Within a very short time, lawyers, civil rights groups, the TUC and so on all rounded on the prime minister who had to withdraw his remarks. Maybe if they had been police officers, secondary school teachers or even politicians it would have been different!

There could be other examples in which an employee's conduct might impinge on the ethos or morally of a particular employment. Conduct relating to the disclosure of trade secrets, competition and so on could be dealt with as breaches of contract. There may be restrictive covenants in an employee's contract in these areas, and in any event, there is an implied duty on an employee not to disclose trade secrets and to act in good faith and fidelity.

When confronted with criminal conduct or alleged criminal conduct outside the employment the employer needs to consider:

▌ What is the nature of the conduct and does this have a bearing on the role performed by the employee? For example, a conviction for theft by a trainee accountant and a conviction for serious violence by a night-club security officer have a direct bearing on their roles.

▌ Will there be an effect on the reputation of the organization? There may already have been adverse publicity, or this may be a legitimate concern. For example, it might be a conviction for assault on a rider during an anti-hunt rally by an employee of a field sports magazine, or a conviction for any offence of indecency by an employee of a school care-home.

▌ Does the incident involve or affect other employees? If an assault was on another employee, this would raise issues about workplace relationships. Assault and stalking activities are relevant here.

▌ Does the criminal conduct undermine the mutual trust and confidence between an employee and employer? This, I would suggest, would depend on the circumstances.

Some employers, usually in sensitive areas such as security or accountancy practices, include a clause in the contract of employment that a conviction for a criminal offence will result in dismissal. This is clear in some ways but could raise questions in areas such as road traffic law, particularly minor offences.

If disciplinary action in relation to an incident of misconduct outside the organization has already taken place without a dismissal, then the organization, in all fairness, cannot subsequently dismiss following the outcome of criminal proceedings unless new evidence becomes apparent. In limited circumstances it might be possible to justify a dismissal for some other substantial reason, such as in relation to a lengthy custodial sentence.

In the case of a conviction for offences committed away from the workplace, a tribunal would consider any adverse connection between the offence and the employment and the nature of the employee's job. 'So long as in some respect or other it (the conduct) affects the employee, or could be thought to be likely to affect the employee, when he is doing his work' was one decision. Criminal conduct will not necessarily make a dismissal fair in every circumstance.

A long remand in custody may well serve to 'frustrate' the contract and justify dismissal (*Kingston* v *British Railways Board* [1984] IRLR 146, CA) even if the employee is subsequently found not guilty. A disciplinary hearing before a criminal trial for an alleged offence outside work should only be held after careful consideration.

One final point in this section is that an employee may be fairly dismissed where they conceal from their employer a criminal conviction under the Rehabilitation of Offenders Act 1974. Whether or not the conviction is 'spent' and the individual is a 'rehabilitated person' under the Act depends on the severity of the sentence and the time that has elapsed since it was imposed. There is a sliding scale contained in the Act and this detail should be considered before taking any disciplinary action.

In short, it is not automatically fair to dismiss an employee convicted of a criminal offence outside work without considering the circumstances.

4

Grievances

GENERAL COMMENTS

Our focus in this chapter is on internal grievances raised by employees, or in certain circumstances, ex-employees. First, it is necessary to mention complaints, which may be from an external source in respect of quality or service provided by the organization. While they need to be addressed, and some will demand an investigation, they are not grievances in the true meaning of the legislation. Case study 5 on recruitment (page 184) is an example. Your organization may have a procedure designed to address external complaints.

Grievances may be received from internal sources relating to actions of individuals or groups within the organization. In either of these scenarios there may be the possibility of discipline implications, and some complaints will need to be investigated as such.

Collective grievances raised by trade unions, consultation groups or staff associations are outside our scope. They seldom raise discipline issues, and as such, do not require to be investigated in the same way. While they do occasionally result in tribunal hearings, they are not covered by the same procedures as individual grievances.

While some grievances may involve a disciplinary allegation, many will relate to treatment of an individual by:

▌ unfair or inconsistent application of existing policies and procedures;
▌ decisions made by managers affecting an individual;
▌ relationship issues within the workplace.

It should be possible to resolve many grievances simply and informally, but some will require investigation by a process similar to that relating to discipline. If it is unclear whether or not an issue raised by an employee is to be treated as a formal grievance, a manager is well advised to take the view that it is a formal grievance until the alternative is established.

I hope I am not being too naïve when I say that the initial mindset when a grievance is received should not be 'Not another whinge!' or 'What are they complaining about now?' It should be that it likely to be a genuine problem and this is an opportunity to put matters right. I genuinely believe that the correct attitude, in the early stages at least, can lead to better outcomes, more issues being dealt with at the lowest level, fewer appeals and a reduced number of tribunal claims. I make this recommendation based on experience, not a desire to appear weak or compliant.

WHY HAVE GRIEVANCE PROCEDURES?

Grievances are concerns, problems or complaints that employees raise with their employers. Grievance procedures are used by employers to deal with employees' grievances in a fair and consistent manner. Employment law requires that a process should be in place to deal with grievances. This is a contractual requirement. A correctly applied grievance procedure is essential to demonstrate to an employee, and maybe later a tribunal, that the employer has behaved appropriately in dealing with the grievance. It is worth pointing out they not only does the policy dictate how grievances are to be dealt with, it will also include how matters can be concluded by progressing to the final decision, following from as many stages as the procedure allows.

In addition to the statutory right for employees to access a grievance procedure, there is an implied duty for employers to 'reasonably and promptly afford a reasonable opportunity to their employees to obtain redress of any grievance they may have' (*WA Goold (Pearmark) Ltd* v *McConnell & anor* [1995] IRLR 516). Thus, in addition to any written terms governing grievance procedures, employees are impliedly entitled to have their grievances dealt with, and any failure on the employer's part to deal with a genuine grievance would potentially give the employee the right to resign and claim constructive dismissal. In fact, some employees submit complex grievances with that very outcome in mind.

The statement of main terms of employment must include:

- any grievance procedure applicable to the employee;
- the name or description of the person with whom the employee can raise a grievance and the manner in which grievances should be raised.

Under the current statutory procedure, employees must follow a three-step process:

- **Step 1.** Inform the employer's line manager of their grievance in writing.
- **Step 2.** Be invited by the employer to a meeting to discuss the grievance (where the right to be accompanied will apply in some circumstances). The employee must take all reasonable steps to attend this meeting, and should be notified in writing of the decision without undue delay.
- **Step 3.** Be given the right to take the matter further if they feel the grievance has not been satisfactorily resolved. The employee must be notified of the final appeal decision.

TRAINING AND AWARENESS

The procedure for informal and formal grievance procedures should be dealt with in any induction process. It is important to ensure that everyone in the organization understands the grievance procedures and that all supervisors, managers, and where they are in place employee representatives, are trained in their use. Employees must be given a copy of the procedures or have ready access to them, for instance on a notice board on the intranet or in a staff handbook.

Any training must be well planned, particularly for people who do not speak English as a first language or who have difficulty with reading.

DRAFTING GRIEVANCE PROCEDURES

ACAS guidelines stress that grievance procedures should make it easy for employees to raise issues with management and should:

- be simple and put in writing;
- enable an employee's line manager to deal informally with a grievance, if possible;
- keep proceedings confidential;
- allow the employee to have a companion at relevant meetings.

The types of issue that may give rise to a grievance include administrative matters such as:

- terms and conditions of employment, such as mobility clauses, granting of annual leave, overtime issues, booking of annual leave;
- working practices, for example flexi-time, allocation of duties;
- the working environment, such as personal protective equipment, working conditions in summer/winter;
- training matters, such as lack of training, unfair allocation;
- health and safety issues generally.

In addition, grievances may relate to more personal matters, including:

- work relations, such as bullying and harassment;
- family-friendly policies, such as granting of parental leave or compassionate leave;
- organizational change and its impact on the individual;
- equal pay issues;
- equality of opportunities generally.

In many organizations, policies will exist specifically for bullying, harassment, discrimination and equality of opportunity. Where separate procedures do exist these should be used instead of the standard grievance procedure.

INFORMAL RESOLUTION

Best practice dictates that procedures should be in place to encourage employees to aim to resolve most grievances informally with their line manager, at the lowest possible level. This has advantages for all workplaces, particularly where there might be a close personal relationship between a manager and an employee. It also has the potential for problems to be resolved quickly. Of course some grievances relate to serious matters and require a formal process. In some a resolution may be beyond the authority of the immediate line manager, or occasionally the complaint is about the line manager's decisions, behaviour or treatment. In these cases the matter should move to the formal procedure.

It is unlikely that an informal grievance will require other than a low-level investigation. It was never intended that this stage should become a bureaucratic procedure; in fact, quite the contrary. However, a prudent manager will make a brief file or diary note of the grievance and their efforts to resolve it. This may be useful if the grievance progresses to a formal stage and is aggravated by a further complaint that the line manager did not address the issue appropriately – which, incidentally, is not unusual!

Dealing with a grievance informally has the potential to save a great deal of organizational effort, have a possible impact on an employee's morale, help to resolve any minor misunderstanding and develop a positive relationship between the employee and the line manager. Unfortunately some line managers are reluctant to make the effort, and actively encourage their staff to commit grievances to paper and a formal process. I recall delivering a consultancy project in a further education college where the accepted tactic was to submit even the most minor grievance to a senior manager in writing. This wasted a great deal of time and was to no one's advantage. If this is the case, senior managers should do whatever they can to discourage it. Of course, it was indicative of the morale within the college at the time.

Line managers do not have to deal with informal grievances instantly; they can make brief enquiries, clarify policies with senior managers and negotiate with team members over a limited period.

My experience is that if you as a manager have made a mistake, a misunderstanding or incorrect application of a company policy resulting in an informal grievance, by far the best policy is to apologize and put matters right. Failing to take this approach often results in a formal grievance. I recommend the adage, 'If you are in a hole, stop digging!'

FORMAL PROCEDURE

If a grievance cannot be settled informally, the employee should raise it formally with their line manager in writing and follow that with a meeting. There are certain occasions when it is not necessary to follow the statutory procedure: for example, if the employee is raising a concern in compliance with the Public Interest Disclosure Act (see later), or a grievance is raised on behalf of at least two employees by an appropriate representative such as an official of an independent trade union (beyond the scope of this book).

GRIEVANCE INVESTIGATIONS

The techniques and tactics covered in the next few chapters are of course applicable to investigating a grievance. However, the time necessary to delve into the background and content of a grievance can vary immensely. The type of grievances requiring some degree of investigation might include:

- issues relating to custom and practice;
- complaints about unfair treatment in allocation of duties;
- complaints about misuse of personal data held by an employer;
- complaints about unfair treatment in terms of application of family-friendly policies, availability of training and so on;
- contractual matters such as changes of workplace or work hours.

Before holding the grievance meeting, a manager may wish to be aware of the background of the grievance and any policies or procedures relevant to the issue under discussion.

Of course, a grievance may be used to raise a discipline allegation against another employee. If this is the case, the complainant should be informed that a discipline investigation will take and they will be expected to cooperate with the process.

EQUAL PAY ACT 1970

One particular type of grievance that will require a special investigation is that relating to equal pay. Here a female employee seeks to claim that her contract is detrimental in some way (usually pay and benefits) when compared with a male employee doing work of equal value. Many of these issues end up in an employment tribunal having started their lives as internal grievances. The 'comparator' must be in the same employment and carrying out 'like or equal value work'. If this is established the employer can raise a 'genuine material factor defence', or of course make an appropriate contractual variation.

We need go no further into the law at this stage other than to say it is important that the investigator interviews the complainant carefully, seeks out consistent decisions within the organization, understands the legal position and submits a realistic report to the senior manager making the ultimate decision. This may be an area in which legal advice is required. An employer must realize that these type of individual grievances can be a preliminary issue leading to a whole series of claims. It is important to get both the procedural process and the decision right.

GRIEVANCE RAISED DURING A DISCIPLINE INVESTIGATION

Occasionally an employee under investigation for an alleged discipline offence, whether suspended from work or not, may seek to raise a grievance. This may be about a variety of issues such as the way they were treated or the selection of an inappropriate manager to undertake the investigation. In most cases, employers are advised to pause or suspend the discipline investigation while the grievance is dealt with. This may not always be possible but it is advisable. However, if this tactic is repeated there may be a suspicion that the employee is seeking to delay or prolong the investigation. In this case a senior manager needs to address the issue as a matter of priority.

It is good practice to address any outstanding grievance before a discipline hearing, particularly if this may result in a dismissal.

GRIEVANCE MEETINGS

On receiving a formal grievance, a manager should invite the employee to a meeting as soon as possible and inform them that they have the right to be accompanied. It is good practice to agree a time and place for the meeting with the employee. It is important that the meeting is not interrupted and that the employee feels the grievance is being treated confidentially. If an employee's companion cannot attend on a proposed date, the employee can suggest another date so long as it is reasonable.

The employee should be invited to explain the complaint, the background and say how they think it could be settled. If the employer representative reaches a point in the meeting where they are not sure how to deal with the grievance or feels that further investigation is necessary, the meeting should be adjourned to get advice or carry out the investigation. The employer should give the grievance careful consideration before responding in writing. Many procedures include timetables for the various stages but these are only guidelines. However, if a guideline timescale is not going to be met the manager should inform the employee of this fact and give an indication of the revised timescale.

Employers must bear in mind that employees presenting a grievance could need support if they are lacking in confidence, if they or their representative are suffering from a disability, unable to read, or in particular, their main language is not English. Supporting an employee through a grievance is good practice and should not be taken as an indication that it will be resolved to their satisfaction.

The law and ACAS guidelines contain an uncommon but specific exemption in that employers and employees are normally expected to go through the statutory grievance procedures unless, and unusually, they have reasonable grounds to believe that by doing so they might be exposed to a significant threat, such as violent, abusive or intimidating behaviour or that they will be harassed. There will always be a certain amount of stress and anxiety for both parties when dealing with grievance cases, but this exemption only applies where the employer or employee reasonably believes that they would come to some serious physical or mental harm, their property or some third party is threatened or the other party has harassed them and this may continue. This, of course, is related to the ability of employees to submit a claim to an employment tribunal without first raising a grievance with their employer. I have personally never dealt with such a situation and I can only imagine it being relevant to a small organization.

Equally, the statutory procedure does not need to be followed if circumstances beyond the control of either party prevent one or more steps being followed within a reasonable period. This will sometimes be the case where there is a long-term illness, the employee is in prison or on a long period of absence abroad, but wherever possible the employer should endeavour to deal with the matter.

WRITTEN RESPONSE

Unless a manager is confident in doing so, there is no obligation to make an immediate response at a grievance meeting. The employer should respond in writing to the employee's grievance within a reasonable time and should let the employee know that they can appeal against the decision if they are not satisfied with the response. What is considered reasonable will vary from organization to organization, but five working days is normally long enough. If it is not possible to respond within five working days the employee should be given an explanation for the delay and told when a response can be expected.

The written response may need to be in some detail, and should contain the reasons a specific decision has been made. The letter should be couched in understandable form and explain the decision and the reasons for it clearly. In some cases, the response may need to include the legal position and the detail of relevant company policies and procedures. If the manager hearing the grievance comes to the conclusion that the employee has been treated wrongly or not in accordance with the company policy, the manager should apologize. There is nothing to lose in this and a great deal to gain. Unfortunately, many employers are reluctant to do so. A failure to apologize after wrongful treatments is quite likely to stimulate an appeal or even a tribunal claim. I know of only one situation in which an apology for a mistake, either personally or on behalf of the organization, resulted in problems for an employer. This relates to admissions of responsibility for personal physical or psychological injury which would be inappropriate without legal advice.

This response is normally in the form of a letter or minutes of the meeting. Practically speaking, the decision after a meeting is not given until there has been time for due consideration, and in these cases a letter is sent.

Many of the concepts and techniques listed above apply to this letter. Bear in mind it could be used as the basis for a claim to an employment tribunal. The response should be concise and well thought out. See the example in the box.

Grievance 1

I was employed as secretary to the finance director prior to taking ordinary maternity leave and three months additional maternity leave. On my return I was not given my old position but that of secretary to the sales director.

Response

By virtue of regulations 18(2) of the Maternity and Parental Leave etc Regulations 1999 an employer is not required to return an employee to the same job, after additional maternity leave, if it is not reasonably practicable to do so. This was the case as a permanent replacement had been appointed to maintain continuity. The post of secretary to the sales director is on the same terms and conditions and, in the circumstances, suitable and appropriate. The grievance is rejected.

Grievance 2

I returned from additional maternity leave on 3 April 2008 and was told that my annual leave for the year 2007/08, which ended on 31 March 2008, has been lost. I know that women on maternity leave are allowed to accrue statutory holiday. I therefore ask for the leave to be granted or payment in lieu thereof.

Response

The company policy on leave – a copy is attached – states that all holiday leave must be taken within the leave year in which it is accrued. The year ended on 31 March 2008 and by that date you had failed to take the outstanding leave accrued during your maternity absence. This means that your leave has been lost. In order to ensure consistency across the company, we are unable to grant this leave. The grievance is rejected.

The letter should go on to inform the employee that she has a right of appeal against the decision. You may feel that this employer is rather mean. However, the point is that a response to a grievance of this nature must be investigated and reviewed carefully. It may involve taking legal advice from human resources or a lawyer, as in this case, or it may involve speaking to witnesses or reviewing documentation. The response to these grievances would not give the employee successful grounds for a claim, unless maybe she could establish that the leave had been granted to other employees returning from maternity leave.

The brief examples should make it apparent that grievances can take a great deal of time to resolve. By no means are all as simple as these, and by no means are all rejected at the end of the review process.

APPEALS

If an employee informs the employer that they are unhappy with the decision after a grievance meeting, the employer should arrange an appeal.

So far as is reasonably practicable the appeal should be with a more senior manager than the one who dealt with the original grievance. In small organizations, even if there is no more senior manager available, another manager should, if possible, hear the appeal. If that is not an option, the person overseeing the case should act as impartially as possible. At the same time as inviting the employee to attend the appeal, the employer should remind the employee of their right to be accompanied at the appeal meeting. As with the first meeting, the employer should write to the employee with a decision on the grievance as soon as possible.

The manager hearing an appeal should also tell the employee if the appeal meeting is the final stage of the grievance procedure. In large organizations there may be a further stage of appeal to a higher level of management, such as a director or board member. However, in smaller firms the first appeal will usually mark the end of the grievance procedure. If a small employer feels that the situation requires it, there is always the option to use the services of an external person to hear an appeal. This should, if at all possible, be after an agreement with the employee. Organizations such as ACAS, Chambers of Commerce or independent HR consultants are able to assist in these matters.

KEEPING RECORDS

It is important, and in the interests of both employer and employee, to keep written records during the grievance process. Records should include:

- the nature of the grievance raised;
- a copy of the written grievance;
- the employer's response;
- action taken;
- reasons for action taken;
- whether there was an appeal and, if so, the outcome;
- subsequent developments.

Records should be treated as confidential and kept in accordance with the Data Protection Act 1998, which gives individuals the right to request and have access to certain personal data. Copies of meeting records should be given to the employee, including any formal minutes that have been taken. In certain circumstances (for example to protect a witness) the employer might withhold some information.

Wherever possible a grievance should be dealt with before an employee leaves the employment. A statutory grievance procedure (the 'modified grievance procedure'), however, applies where an employee has already left employment, the standard procedure has not been commenced or completed before the employee left employment and both parties agree in writing that it should be used instead of the standard statutory procedure. Under the modified procedure the employee should write to the employer setting out the grievance as soon as possible after leaving employment and the employer must write back setting out its response. If there is no agreement to use the modified procedure and a written response, a meeting with the ex-employee will be necessary – this is unusual. However, in these circumstances the same rules regarding a companion apply as during employment and in discipline matters (that it is only permissible to be accompanied by a workplace colleague or a trade union official). This said, employers should exercise common sense in respect of people who are vulnerable by any criteria, or those whose first language is not English.

WHISTLEBLOWING

Another area of law cannot be ignored as it can create a need for an investigation very similar to that of a grievance, and in some cases a discipline hearing. This is the special type of grievance commonly known as 'whistleblowing'.

In simple terms whistleblowing is about providing protection to employees from being dismissed or penalized in any way for disclosing information about the organization in which they work. This could be regarding dangers to health and safety, dangers to the environment, miscarriage of justice or financial malpractice. These provisions are contained in the Public Interest Disclosure Act 1998 which, as well as introducing particular rights for employees, included agency workers, home workers, trainees and contractors who disclose information about wrongdoing by the employer.

Providing the specific rules are followed, this law overrides the implied contractual duty of confidentiality employees owe to their employer.

What is a disclosure?

Whistleblowing is not common but employers need to be aware of the specific circumstances in which it can be used and the risk to which they are exposed if they fail to protect the employee providing the information. In order to be protected under the whistleblowing provisions, a disclosure made by an employee must be 'qualifying'. The employee making the disclosure must have a 'reasonable belief' that the information tends to show that one of the six failures (listed below) has occurred, is occurring or is likely to occur. It is not necessary for the information itself to be true provided the employee had a reasonable belief at the time of making the relevant allegations. If the information turns out to be false, this could be critical when considering disciplinary action.

A qualifying disclosure is the disclosure of information which in the reasonable belief of the employee shows one or more of the following types of wrongdoing:

▌ that a criminal offence has been committed, is being committed or is likely to be committed (for example corruption in the provision of services to a public body, use of illegal foreign workers or fraud, systematic evasion of value added tax or national insurance contributions);

▌ that a person failed, is failing or is likely to fail to comply with any legal requirement with which they are obliged to comply (for example tax declarations, movement of nuclear materials);

▌ that a miscarriage of justice has occurred, is occurring or is likely to occur (for example an employer changing drivers' names to avoid speeding penalties);

▌ that the health and safety of any individual (including another employee) has been, is being or is likely to be endangered (for example, inappropriate use of certain chemicals);

▌ that the environment has been, is being or is likely to be damaged (for example pollution, unlawful discharge into a water course);

▌ that information tending to show any matter falling within the five points above has been, is being or is likely to be deliberately concealed.

The circumstances must also satisfy the following conditions in order to be a protected disclosure:

▌ The employee must be acting in good faith.

▌ The employee must believe that the information and any allegation contained in it are true, and the belief must be reasonable.

▌ The employee must not make the disclosure for the purposes of personal gain (for example for media payments).

▌ It must be reasonable for the employee to make the disclosure in all the circumstances of the case.

▌ A disclosure will not be a qualifying disclosure where the person making the disclosure thereby commits a criminal offence (such as theft of documents, or breaking into premises).

Making the disclosure

An employee should, in the first instance, raise the matter with their employer. However, in exceptional circumstances, listed below, they can make the disclosure to one of the specific people:

▌ The employee holds a reasonable belief that they will be victimized by their employer if they tell their employer.

▌ There is no prescribed person to tell and they reasonably believe that the evidence will be concealed or destroyed if they tell their employer.

▌ They have already told their employer or a prescribed person. Such a subsequent disclosure only has to be substantially the same as that which was previously disclosed and can be expanded to include information about any action taken or not taken by any person as a result of the previous disclosure.

In such a case the disclosure can only be made to specific categories of people. These include 'prescribed persons', such as the Health and Safety

Executive, Charity Commissioners Data Protection Registrar, Rail Regulator, or a legal adviser. Only if the matter is not resolved internally or by a prescribed body or person can the employee report it to someone else, which could be the media.

Suffering a detriment

If a disclosure is received and once it has been established that there has been a protected disclosure, it is then necessary to determine whether or not the employee has been subjected to any detriment or whether any unlawful victimization has taken place. This obviously includes dismissal but also disciplinary action, lack of promotion and a poor reference. Even a threat could amount to a detriment. The legislation was clearly brought in to cover serious issues, like the major disasters of the 1990s, but also applies to lesser concerns. For example, a support worker in a residential home was harassed by another support worker because she had reported to management a resident's complaint about the latter (Cumbria County Council *v* Carlisle-Morgan [2007] UKEAT/0323/06; 827 IDS Brief 8, EAT) or a junior NHS manager might report inappropriate payments to a resigning NHS director.

Internal investigations

For our purposes, the only situations to explore a little further are:

▌ where a disclosure has been made to an employer;
▌ when an employee alleges that they have been subject to a 'detriment' (such as victimization) after making a disclosure;
▌ when a disclosure made to an outside person or body is alleged not to have been made in good faith.

In these cases, an internal investigation is necessary and the tactics covered in these chapters are relevant. This type of investigation will be complex and sensitive. It could be subject to later scrutiny by a tribunal, court or other external body. The manager selected to undertake the investigation should, if at all possible, be experienced. While we deal with evidence gathering later, it seems critical in these cases that the evidence is secured and protected immediately.

Disciplinary action

The law is complex and allows disclosures to be made to a variety of specified official agencies or individuals, in addition to or as an alternative to the employer. If the employee is found to have not acted in 'good faith' this will bring the need for a disciplinary investigation and maybe action such as dismissal.

This area may seem to be at the extreme edge of our topic but it does have the potential to place an employer at risk if it does not respond to a disclosure as defined above or takes action against the employee providing the information. In most circumstances it will necessitate an investigation and report. It is important an employer acts properly in these circumstances.

ORGANIZATIONAL REVIEW

Some grievances may suggest that all is not right within the organization or a particular section, or process, or even with a particular manager. Employers should not miss the opportunity to review the issues after a grievance, particularly if it was found in favour of the employee. We discuss reflective practice elsewhere in the book and it is an important concept. Organizations and individuals need to develop the ability to learn from experiences, and this includes from a process that was successful as well as one that was less so or even failed.

5

Suspensions

WHAT SUSPENSION IS

There are several circumstances in which an employer can suspend an employee from work, including certain medical conditions or specific circumstances related to pregnancy. In some circumstances an employee can be sent on so-called 'garden leave'. Within our topic of discipline the option exists to suspend an employee, or even a group of employees, while an investigation is carried out following an allegation of serious misconduct. Suspension is a formal and neutral process, recognized in employment law, whereby an employee is removed from the workplace. Employees are relieved of their duties, any keys, passes or computer access, and are instructed not to attend their workplace and in most cases not to contact their work colleagues (although is notoriously difficult to 'police') without specific permission.

The position regarding suspension from work to facilitate a discipline investigation is succinctly set out in the ACAS code of practice:

> In certain cases, for example in cases involving gross misconduct, where relationships have broken down or there are risks to an employer's property or responsibilities to other parties, consideration should be given to a brief period of suspension with full pay whilst unhindered investigation is conducted. Such a suspension should only be imposed after careful consid-

eration and should be reviewed to ensure it is not unnecessarily protracted. It should be made clear that the suspension is not considered a disciplinary action.

Suspension in these circumstances does not, in itself, carry any inference of guilt. However, try telling the suspended employee that! Deciding to suspend an employee is a serious step, but if conducted in a fair and consistent manner, it carries little risk to the employer. A precedent has been set that suspension without reasonable and proper cause could be a breach of the implied duty of mutual trust and confidence between employer and employee. In one case (_Gogay_ v _Hertfordshire County Council_ [2000] IRLR 703, Ct of Appeal) a care worker was suspended following obscure allegations made by a child with learning difficulties. The allegations were subsequently discovered to be unfounded but the employee subsequently developed clinical depression and was unable to work.

SUSPENSION CHECKLIST

In order to investigate a complaint of serious or gross misconduct during the course of any disciplinary process, an employer may suspend an employee from their duties but it must be on full pay and with full entitlement to all other contractual benefits such as a company car, gymnasium membership, or health insurance, for as long as the employer considers it necessary to carry out a proper investigation of the complaint.

When looking at whether to suspend, an employer should consider:

- the instructions and procedures that may be set out in the discipline policy (if so these should be followed);
- the severity of the allegation(s), particularly if the allegation amounts to serious misconduct (it would be highly unusual to consider suspension for allegations of simple misconduct);
- the impact that any failure to suspend might have on the reputation of the organization, for example allegations of financial improprieties in an accountancy firm or allegations of assault in school;
- any serious suggestion that the employee against whom the allegation is made could interfere with the investigation, any potential witnesses, the gathering of evidence, or there is a risk to property or other people.

There is an alternative in some cases, if the size and complexity if the organization allows, and this is to transfer the person to duties that are unconnected with the alleged offence or any complainant, maybe at a different location.

A decision to suspend may need to be made at a specified level in the organization. It is not uncommon for a manager to decide to 'send an employee home' until a formal decision to suspend can be made. In this case the same checklist should be used.

A period of suspension should be for as short a period as possible while the case is being investigated. There may be guidelines in your discipline policy on time limits and reviews of the suspension decision. Suspension should ideally be for a few days or weeks but can, in complex cases, be for many months, particularly where the investigation involves complex financial allegations. In my personal experience periods of suspension have been from one day to many months. The longest I can recall was for 18 months, with allegations of financial impropriety and racial harassment, and was interspersed with periods of unavailability as a result of a stress-related illness. Although we shall mention this later, consider the pressure put on the 'independent manager' running the investigation at the same time as running their own department – having someone on suspension can increase this pressure.

While suspension does allow tempers to cool, it also carries a stigma than can be attached to an employee who is later found to be innocent. In some organizations suspension decisions are made quickly while in others there seems to be a reluctance to do so, even when it is patently necessary. The four considerations listed above would seem to be at the core of any decision to suspend.

There is one final practical point on this matter. Managers or investigators must be aware that as soon as a person is aware of an investigation they may see it to their advantage to remove, erase/delete/reformat, destroy or otherwise take from the grasp of the investigator evidence that would support the allegation. This could be in paper form, including company records, or electronic data.

SPECIAL CIRCUMSTANCES INVOLVING THE COMPLAINANT OR VICTIM

Occasionally, the circumstances of the allegation or complaint create a situation in which it may be necessary to remove the complainant from the workplace for their emotional or physical safety. If this step is necessary – and it will be only in exceptional cases – the use of paid special leave would seem to be the appropriate administration process to use.

In some cases, the investigation reveals that the complaint or allegation was false or malicious. The circumstances may suggest that a further investigation ought to be carried into the conduct of the 'complainant'. These cases are rare but not unknown.

SUSPENSION PROCEDURES

When the decision is made it is important that a formal process is followed:

1. Your policy may require this decision to be given to the employee after they have been offered the opportunity to be accompanied. This is good practice in any event.
2. Tell the employee exactly why they are being suspended. It may not be possible to inform them of all the matters under investigation at the time of the suspension, but enough should be known to indicate the general area. Full details of the allegations should be supplied as soon as they are known or available.
3. The suspension should be accompanied by a formal letter. An example is included in the Appendix to this book.
4. The letter should contain:
   a) The general nature of the allegations under investigation.
   b) The fact that the employee should not enter the workplace without prior authorization.
   c) The fact that they should not contact any member of staff without prior authorization (this may be difficult to enforce with contact between friends away from work).
   d) The name and contact details of a person within the organization who has the responsibility to maintain contact with the suspended employee. (It should be remembered that the suspended employee is innocent until found guilty and the employer still has contractual responsibilities towards all its staff.)
   e) The date, or period of time, when the decision to suspend will be subject to review – this may be governed by your policy.
5. The employee should be informed that they will be called in for a disciplinary interview as soon as possible.
6. It may help to reinforce that fact that suspension on full pay is not a sanction before the disciplinary interview but is a 'neutral act'. (The point has been made that some will find this hard to accept!)

After allowing the employee to retrieve personal items from their workplace they should be escorted from the premises. IT network access should be suspended and most organizations have remote access to achieve this. This process should be carried out as sensitively as possible.

RESPONSIBILITIES DURING SUSPENSION

During any such period of suspension:

- The employer will be under no obligation to provide any work.
- The suspended employee will usually be required to stay away from the company's premises and to have no contact with any employees, customers, clients or suppliers.
- Some disciplinary policies allow contact to the extent that it is necessary to enable the suspended employee to investigate or defend any disciplinary charges or grievances brought against them.
- The suspended employee will continue to be bound by all of the obligations under their contract such as the duty of confidentiality and good faith to the employer.

The employer has a responsibility, as soon as the full details are known, to inform the employee of the allegations against them and, in most cases the name of the investigating officer and the discipline officer (the manager who will hear any discipline hearing).

The nature of the allegation(s) and the circumstances of the suspended employee may require that a degree of employee support be offered during this period. Personnel/ HR or welfare officers usually take this role but in smaller organizations it may need to be an independent manager. It should be this person who liaises with the suspended employee with regard to any requests they may make to speak to witnesses or discover evidence necessary for their defence. While this should be carefully controlled it would be contrary to natural justice to fail to allow an employee to adequately prepare a defence against any allegations.

FAILURE TO FOLLOW TERMS OF SUSPENSION

It is not unknown for an employee to breach the conditions of suspension, for example to attend the workplace or contact witnesses when told not to do so. The action to be taken will, of course, depend on the circumstances. As an employer, you are not able, except in the unlikely circumstances that the contract of employment so allows, to stop the pay of the suspended employee as this would give the employee cause for action against the employer.

Any such action on the part of the suspended employee may amount to a further discipline charge of misconduct. However, they may anticipate the worst and have little to lose. Conversely, they may be innocent and may see any actions they take as 'fighting for their job'!

In these circumstances, you should check whether the employee was told not to contact anyone verbally or in writing. If verbally, do you have the notes to back you up? There may have been a misunderstanding and in such a case it might be sensible to remind the employee, in writing, that this is not allowed and that any further contravention of the conditions could expose them to additional disciplinary action.

If the outcome of the original investigation is dismissal, and any appeal is disallowed, there is no point in pursuing the contravention. If the outcome is a withdrawal of the allegations or a penalty lower than dismissal, a decision will have to be made to continue or not. I would suggest that, if the allegations are unfounded or unsubstantiated (more of these terms later), any further action would be heavy-handed and oppressive.

RESIGNATION DURING SUSPENSION OR INVESTIGATION

It is always open to an employee to resign and terminate their contract of employment by giving notice. The contract will, of course, contain the terms of notice necessary for this action. This point is that an employer cannot prevent an employee resigning and, furthermore, it is not uncommon for an employee so to do when they perceive the 'tide flowing strongly against them'. The employer must be satisfied that the resignation is voluntary. An employee can resign immediately, without giving notice, and breach their contract of employment. If this does occur it will only be in exceptional circumstances that an employer would seek remedies for this breach at court as it would need to establish a specific loss due to the resignation without notice. In most cases the costs set against what might be recovered if successful make this a 'non-starter'.

In the event of a resignation, it is good practical advice to complete the investigation (unless it would be excessively onerous and costly) and file it away. There is an outside chance that the ex-employee could take action after leaving and the evidence you gather in the investigation may be useful.

'PERSUADING' AN EMPLOYEE UNDER INVESTIGATION TO RESIGN

It is not uncommon for managers and employers to see the cost of an investigation or the impact it may have on the workplace as a negative factor. They may even feel that disciplinary action would reflect poorly on them personally or the perception of the company in its particular marketplace. Occasionally this leads them to consider suggesting to an employee that they should consider submitting their resignation rather than 'suffer' the investigation, discipline hearing and possible dismissal. It could even be suggested that their efforts to find further employment would be better in light of a resignation than a disciplinary dismissal, and this is doubtless true.

This practice is relatively common in public sector bodies when allegations are made against senior members of staff. The politics within these organizations are outside the scope of this book.

On the other hand, an investigator may find that a trade union representative will advise an employee that resignation would be a sensible option in the particular circumstances in which they find themselves. This can occur during a discipline hearing if a stage is reached when the evidence becomes overwhelming.

However, anyone considering a resolution via this route should do so with care, and should never proceed without a properly drafted and signed compromise agreement. In simple terms, a compromise agreement is a legally binding contract in which the parties concerned agree not to take action or issue proceedings. There are specific rules to follow. In our example, it would be used to prevent the employee wishing to resign from later claiming constructive unfair dismissal. It may involve a payment and other conditions, such as an agreed reference. ACAS can also negotiate similar agreements.

CONSTRUCTIVE DISMISSAL

It is my aim not to delve too deeply into the law but remain at the level of practical advice and guidance. However, certain terms need a little explanation and this is one of them. Constructive dismissal is based on the fact that an employee resigns, with or without giving notice, because of a breach of the employment contract by the employer. The breach of contract, or in fact the anticipated breach, must be fundamental to the contract, more than just unreasonable behaviour on the part of the employer. Lawyers call this a 'repudiatory' breach. Examples include arbitrarily reducing pay, refusing contractual rights like a discipline hearing, failing to investigate allegations of sexual harassment and similar serious matters.

Pressurizing an employee to resign would most likely be considered a breach of the implied right to mutual trust and confidence, and warrant an employee to resign and claim constructive dismissal. This point of the whole process is that, under normal circumstances, an employee cannot make a claim to an employment tribunal of unfair dismissal unless they can prove they were dismissed. The ability to establish a 'constructive' dismissal would allow a complaint to be made.

MANAGING THE GRAPEVINE

It is extremely difficult to keep any disciplinary activity secret in an organization unless it is very large or well dispersed. The story, or a version of it, does seem to get out and modern electronic communications make it much easier. While you may want to keep the investigation under wraps, this may prove difficult. There are several valid reasons why you may wish to 'manage' the information in the 'public domain', including:

- Natural justice requires that the employee under investigation should be treated as innocent until proven guilty.
- Too much information may have a negative impact on your evidence-gathering activities – although in a few cases it can have the opposite effect.
- If members of your staff are not given some information they tend to make up a 'good story' – many senior police investigators try to get their side of the story into the media before others claim the first headlines, and this is a good tactic.
- There is a duty of care on the employer to protect staff who have made allegations, particularly in areas such as sexual or racial harassment, bullying or assault, and also those against whom allegations have been made.

The circumstances of the investigation and the allegations will dictate what, if anything, could be said. However, there is a clear need to make some attempt to correct negative or false rumours.

Some large organizations use suspension frequently and reinstatements are quite common. In these cases the stigma is less intense. In others, that suspend employees infrequently, the position can be quite different.

In all circumstances, the investigator must not take any decision regarding publicizing details of the investigation that could prejudice the outcome of it or any subsequent discipline hearing. It may be worth discussing this matter with the employee under investigation and their representative. However, in most cases the best advice is to maintain secrecy and confidentiality as long as possible.

REINTRODUCTION AFTER SUSPENSION

If an employee is suspended and the investigation fails to substantiate the charges, the allegations are found to be malicious or a penalty short of dismissal is imposed at a discipline hearing the employee will need to be reinstated and reintroduced into the workplace. This must be done as soon as possible. The employer will need to remember its obligations under the contract of employment, in particular that the employer must not behave in a manner likely to destroy or seriously damage the relationship of mutual trust and confidence with the employee. Failure to do so could give the employee grounds to resign and claim constructive unfair dismissal.

The reintroduction should be carefully planned, especially if the suspension has been over a period of several months. In extreme cases, updated training and a new induction course may be necessary. A return to the same work unit from which an allegation emanated may be problematic. In any event, the views of the returning employee need to be taken into consideration.

Some employees will find it impossible to return, and negotiations need to be undertaken to manage their resignation in such a way as to mitigate the possibility of litigation, by use of a compromise agreement and maybe an agreed payment.

One of the most difficult situations is that in which the staff know or believe the returning employee to be guilty, but for a variety of reasons the person was found not to be so at the discipline hearing. This could be because of procedural issues, reluctant witnesses and so on. It is a fact of life that, in some cases, 'not guilty', or unsubstantiated in our terminology, is not always the same as 'innocent'.

In most circumstances, however, the return can be made with little more than the support of the immediate line manager. The need for the manager to 'keep an eye on the situation' will remain, particularly to prevent any victimization against a complainant, witness or the person against whom the original allegations were made.

6

Capability

POTENTIALLY FAIR DISMISSAL

The Employment Rights Act 1996 states that no employee should be dismissed unfairly, and lists six potentially fair reasons for dismissal, which are:

- the capability or qualifications of the employee for performing work of the kind they were employed to do;
- the employee's conduct – you might recognize this as 'misconduct';
- redundancy – do not fall into the trap of using this procedure as an alternative to discipline or capability and leave the way clear for an unfair dismissal claim;
- a legal restriction making continued employment impossible: for example, a driver loses their licence or a doctor is 'struck off' the medical register;
- retirement, a formal procedure recently added to the list;
- some other substantial reason justifying the dismissal of an employee; that is, a potentially serious issue such as a breakdown in relationships or a significant personality clash.

We shall be dealing with issues related to conduct in some detail, and the other reasons are outside our scope. However, many employers and managers seem to confuse discipline and capability. When planning this book it seemed appropriate to include capability procedures and dismissals. You will recall that 'conduct', in general terms, amounts to behaviour that is unacceptable in the employment context – in common parlance, 'misconduct'.

The term 'capability' is defined as being 'assessed by reference to skill, aptitude, health or any other physical or mental quality'. A dismissal on the grounds that an employee lacks the required skills or aptitudes to perform the job for which they were employed will be potentially fair, as will a dismissal on the grounds of genuine ill-health or injury. This is, of course, provided a fair procedure is followed.

This chapter deals with managerial action and, if appropriate, dismissal for capability on grounds that an employee lacks the required skills or aptitudes. Actions to deal with long-term sickness and physical or mental disabilities are beyond our range, other than to say that they are complex areas and should not be tackled without professional advice, particularly if the question of disability arises.

This confusion is not made any easier by the fact that many organizations include 'conduct' and 'capability' in the same discipline policy and procedure. Misconduct is a conscious act, whether minor or serious, and is a discipline issue. Capability, or more clearly lack of capability, is unintentional, and unless it can be resolved by training and support, is permanent. It is not a disciplinary issue and there is the difference!

The advice is this chapter is intended to be practical and useful. It is not good practice to use discipline procedures when an employee lacks skills and attributes. Furthermore, it could lead to an unfair dismissal claim.

GENERAL CONSIDERATIONS

Incompetence giving rise to an unacceptable level of performance at work comes within the ordinary meaning of lack of capability. When it becomes apparent, action is likely to be required in the interests of the business, and also perhaps in the interests of the employee. It is not unfair to dismiss an employee if the employer reasonably and honestly believes the employee to be incompetent. However, this must be carried out after proper appraisals, support and warnings.

Poor performance by supervisors and managers will have a similar if not worse impact, and requires attention from senior management. The temptation to support a manager at a lower level whose competence is causing problems just because they are a manager may lead to disastrous consequences for the business, even if it selected the manager in the first place!

In all cases where management genuinely believes that an employee's performance is inadequate, the primary objective should be to get them to improve to the required standard, with dismissal as very much the last resort. Only if discussions, training, counselling or mentoring and the other steps fail to produce the desired improvement should dismissal for lack of capability be the remedy.

However, and as stated above, a distinction must be drawn between innate incompetence and lack of performance. For example, a wilful refusal to work satisfactorily, such as being careless or lazy, would become a disciplinary issue. A good clue to which is which, although not fool-proof, is whether an employee had previously worked satisfactorily but has apparently dropped in performance, or they have never reached the required standard. I use the phrase 'not foolproof' because issues like stress, failing eyesight, bullying and stress can reduce performance, and are definitely not discipline issues from the perspective of the victim.

INITIAL ACTION

Every manager who needs to deal with poor performance faces the dual challenges of recognizing the problem and having to describe to the employee concerned how they are failing to cope adequately with the work. This action certainly fits into the category of a 'difficult conversation'.

The problem can manifest itself as a discipline issue. For example, I recall a man who got through a recruitment process and was disciplined for failing to follow written procedures. It was only later that we realized he could hardly read! It is not uncommon for colleagues to support and protect employees who are not developing as they should in a particular job. This is creditable in some regards but does not help in the long term.

Remember, employees are entitled to know exactly what is expected of them and to what standard. Ideally this should have been covered in the induction procedure and reinforced from time to time.

Immediately an apparent lack of capability is suspected, the manager should try to identify the extent to which the individual's performance is considered deficient. The assessment must be as specific as possible. General terms like 'You aren't showing enough enthusiasm for your work', 'Your general approach leaves much to be desired', 'You're lazy', will not help the employee to know how they can improve their performance.

If a trade union is recognized by an employer, early consultation with the employee's representative can lead to other assistance being given to an employee to improve. Such consultation may also prove to have been useful if the employee fails to improve sufficiently and is dismissed: the union will have been made fully aware of the reason for dismissal and of the circumstances leading up to the decision. It can be valuable to the union and to the employer for there to have been an early exchange of information about the employee's shortcomings. The employee must of course agree to union involvement.

Reliance on an annual appraisal or review will not in itself be sufficient to support a decision to dismiss for lack of capability, although the content of such reports will be material to any case of dismissal for inadequate performance. A fair appraisal scheme should serve to highlight any problems an employee may be experiencing.

BORDERLINE CASES

Before dealing with the safe procedure to follow, I would ask you to consider the borderline case. Blatant misconduct is reasonably clear, as is an obvious lack of competence, and in each case the correct procedure should be followed. However, there are several areas that are not so easy to categorize, for example:

- inflexibility and a reluctance to adopt new skills;
- persistent carelessness;
- inaccurate work;
- lack of concentration.

While these issues are not normally seen as serious misconduct, are they evidence of misconduct or a lack of competence? The first step is clear. The manager should discuss the issues with the employee, and support the discussion by describing the unacceptable behaviour. This is best achieved by sticking to facts rather than opinions. The employee should be made aware of the required standard of performance or behaviour, and asked for a commitment to improve. This should not be a bureaucratic process; a brief diary note should suffice followed by a period of monitoring.

An improvement is an achievement in two ways. It reveals that the employee is capable of delivering the required standard and it benefits the whole work unit. The employee should be congratulated and a period of casual monitoring should ensure matters do not revert to the original unacceptable level of performance. The other benefit is that any fallback in performance can usually be regarded as a failure in conduct rather than capability.

It is not always as simple as this may suggest. If the performance continues at the unacceptable level or any improvement is still not enough to reach the required standard, it is safer to take the position of dealing with it as a capability issue and follow the procedure described in the next few paragraphs.

CAPABILITY CHECKLIST

When dealing with a suspected case of incompetence (capability), an employer must follow the agreed procedure carefully. The key stages are described in this chapter. While it is unnecessary to give warnings in the event of gross incompetence or unsuitability (examples have included the incompetent landing of an aircraft resulting in extremely serious damage (*Alidair Ltd* v *Taylor* [1976] IRLR 420, EAT) or incompetence that has serious economic consequences (for example, deliberate or reckless incompetence leading to a loss of a whole production batch), these cases are few and far between.

An employer should be slow to dismiss upon these grounds without first telling the employee of the respects in which they are failing to do their job adequately, warning them of the possibility or likelihood of dismissal on this ground, and giving them an opportunity to improve their performance.

We have already agreed that management's aim should be to encourage the employee to improve their performance to an acceptable level. Where performance can be measured against standards (as may be easier with production line workers or sales representatives, as opposed to other classes of employees whose output is less specific), it should be possible to assess by how far the employee is performing below standard and to ascertain when the employee improves to the standard required. For jobs where standards are difficult to prescribe, such as in management, the employer has the task of assessing on reasonable grounds whether the employee's performance is acceptable.

Line managers should be aware of the output of their staff and should be in a position to notice indicators of under-performance. Questions may include:

- What are the indications that the employee is not measuring up to the requirements of the job? Are there parts of the job not being done? This may be based on performance figures, as mentioned above, or on observation of behaviour, commitment and output.
- Have there been complaints about or criticisms of the employee's work from colleagues, suppliers, customers, members of the public or even subordinates? This can be picked up by grievances, issues with appraisals and so on.
- Does the manager's own observation of the employee at work indicate dissatisfaction with their performance?
- Has the employee asked for help to overcome a problem?
- Have there been delays in finishing work or frequent inaccuracies where this is important?

The initial stages of a procedure for responding to inadequate perform-ance, and the suspicion of incompetence, are likely to be conditioned by the answers to those questions and to the extent to which the deficiencies in the employee's performance are manifesting themselves. You will have already taken the initial action in raising the issue with your employee. This will undoubtedly be one of the more difficult conversations we have discussed elsewhere.

The initial action mentioned above is not really part of the procedure; it is a preliminary step that may result in a resolution of the problem. However, if this is not the case, here is a recommended procedure. I make no apology for included this in some detail as it is a potentially difficult area:

1. An informal discussion with the employee, focusing in particular on how the employee is thought not to be performing satisfactorily. Does the employee accept that there is a problem? Will the employee respond to constructive suggestions to bring about an improvement? Responses from employees in these circumstances may fall into one of four categories:

   a) The employee accepts that there is a problem and leaves it to the manager to suggest what could be done (eg better instruction on how to do the work, training or retraining, closer supervision, a move to other work, or a mentoring programme). This passive response by the employee is more likely to occur when the employee is unable to cope with a technical problem, or perhaps lacks sufficient knowledge to do the work adequately.

   b) The employee expresses doubt about whether there is a problem, but indicates willingness to respond to any suggestions the manager may make. This leaves it to the manager to suggest possible solutions, discuss the merits of them with the employee and seek the employee's agreement to the most appropriate. In these cases, observed facts might help convince the employee of the problem.

   c) The employee acknowledges the problem and asks for help to resolve it.

   d) The employee denies the existence of any problem, despite the facts presented to them (in which case stage 3 below will usually be omitted).

2. The manager should make and keep an informal note of the date, time and conclusions reached (if any) for their own use later if the need to refer back to this initial conversation arises.

3. The type of reaction envisaged in 1(c) above, and to some extent in 1 (b), may require a non-threatening and non-critical approach by the

manager with the aim of helping the employee to find a solution, with the manager trying to unearth as many aspects as possible of the problem, as perceived by the employee.

4.   An employee's initial response coming within (1) above, after any discussion as outlined in (3), should be followed by arrangements to monitor the employee's continuing performance, with the observations being recorded. This may well be the responsibility of the employee's immediate supervisor, but the manager should also try to support it with additional personal observation of the employee's work. The manager's aim should be for the employee's performance to be monitored and assessed as objectively as possible and as frequently as appropriate, bearing in mind the nature of the employee's duties and the length of time it would be reasonable to allow for improvement.

5.   The manager should consider whether to consult the employee's trade union representative, if any, about the steps being taken to persuade the employee to improve.

6.   If there is failure to improve or continued unsatisfactory performance, the employee should be invited to a formal interview to discuss the matter and informed that there will then be an opportunity to put forward an explanation, either in person or through a representative.

7.   The employee should be reminded of the earlier informal discussion(s) and of the steps taken to encourage improvement, and be told as precisely as possible of the complaints about their performance. If any explanation offered is not accepted, a formal written caution in writing should be given to the employee as soon after the interview as possible. It should inform the employee that their job may be at risk if satisfactory performance is not achieved and sustained.

8.   Following the issue of the formal caution, action in accordance with (4) above should continue as appropriate.

9.   If the employee's improvement following the formal warning is insufficient to enable them to be regarded as capable of doing the work they are employed to do, the manager should:

   a)   Consider whether alternative employment can be offered to the employee. This does not necessarily have to be equivalent employment.

   b)   If this is acceptable, make the offer in writing, explaining why it is being made and the possible consequences of refusing it. Give the employee sufficient time to consider the offer and, if so wishing, to discuss it with their employee representative.

10. If no offer of alternative employment is made, or if one has been made and rejected by the employee, a further formal interview with the

employee will be appropriate. Again, the employee should be informed of it in advance and the reasons for it, and at the meeting the history of the case should be gone through and the employee's explanations listened to and considered before a decision is taken whether to allow further time for improvement, backed by a further warning or caution.

11. If dismissal is decided upon, it should be with notice, or with pay in lieu of notice.

12. At the time notice is given, the employee should be told of their right of appeal. Although lack of capability is not a disciplinary offence, the normal procedure should be to allow the employee in this position the same avenue of appeal as would be available against an unfavourable disciplinary decision.

One test of whether concern about an employee's inadequate performance is expressed with sufficient clarity is to ask, 'From what is being said, does the employee know precisely what the grounds for complaint are about their perceived difficulty?' If the answer is 'No', the matters being brought to the employee's attention should be better defined – set out in everyday language.

Employees who are the subject of any stages of the procedure and whose response has not produced the required improvement should not receive personal copies of general letters from management or directors which could be construed as congratulating them personally on their contribution to the work of the department or the organization during the preceding year, 'period of great difficulty and/or pressure', and so on.

I have seen an instance in which an employee who had been undergoing the formal stage of a capability procedure received a 'middle-of-the-road' staff appraisal. The manager, somewhat surprisingly, said he did not link the two processes. In fact, one can undermine the other. If an employee is under a formal capability assessment the normal appraisal process should be suspended.

CHANGES IN WORKING TECHNIQUES

Dismissal on grounds that an employee is not capable of acquiring new techniques which, within the terms of the contract of employment, they can be expected or required to perform (such as a computerized system, new machinery, etc) may not be fair unless:

▌ Suitable training has been offered and has been either refused or, if undertaken, has not been completed or has not resulted in the employee becoming sufficiently capable of doing the job.

▌ At least one formal written warning or formal caution in writing has been issued. If training has been undertaken, a warning should be related to the period following completion of the training.

▌ The possibility of alternative employment has been considered, and if offered, has been rejected.

▌ The employee's views on the matter have been heard and considered.

If an employee finds difficulty in dealing with new techniques, and despite prolonged support they are unable to cope, an employer could offer alternative employment in a different area. This could be offered as an alternative to dismissal and could be at different terms and conditions (that is, lower pay). It would need the agreement of the employee and the continuity of employment, their service, would continue.

DENIALS OF INADEQUATE PERFORMANCE

An employee who does not accept that their performance at work is inadequate is unlikely to respond constructively to persuasion to improve. This type of response can justify shortening the period which might otherwise be allowed for improvement, but it will not reduce the need to provide the employee with formal opportunities to offer an explanation and for management to listen to and consider what may be said.

Employees who react with 'everyone's out of step but me' may resent any criticism, actual or implied, of their performance. A common response is to invoke the grievance procedure. If this occurs, management should ensure that access to the process is provided with the minimum delay, and there is also minimum delay while the stages of the grievance procedure are being gone through. If the employee's grievance is held to be ill founded, the procedure should continue.

INADEQUATE PERFORMANCE AFTER PROMOTION

It is not uncommon to find that a promoted employee proves incapable of satisfactorily carrying out the new range of responsibilities. They may have been competent in the previous job but are deficient at the higher level. You may recall the potential problems in this area in the chapter on proactive discipline. It is essential to give the employee the necessary training for the job to which they have been promoted, and many employers do not do this or leave it too late. Consideration of alternative employment for the unsatisfactory promoted employee may involve offering the old job back at the lower graded level (if it is still vacant), or some other post at the level from which they were promoted. If the employee is dismissed and a claim follows, the employer's position will be stronger if it has given the employee the necessary training for the responsibilities of the new post, or has offered such training only for it to be refused or not completed satisfactorily. Unfortunately, it is not uncommon for employers to promise training during a recruitment process and never, for whatever reason, get around to providing it.

The promotion of employees whose ability to cope with their new responsibilities is inadequate is more likely to arise when long-serving employees are promoted from relatively low levels in the organization. If the intention is to reward them for their long and faithful service, the employer will be reluctant indeed to contemplate dismissing them for the inadequate performance they display after promotion. This emphasizes the fact that it may be preferable, where it is decided that such an employee must be removed from their job, not just to offer the alternative of a job at the previous level, but actively to persuade the employee to accept it. If the employee rejects the offer and resigns, they may be entitled to regard this as a constructive unfair dismissal, although if the matter has been considerately handled by the employer, the employee's chances of a successful claim should be remote.

Promotion on a trial or acting basis can enable an otherwise unsatisfactory promotion to be avoided by returning the employee to their substantive level if they are found not to be coping satisfactorily with the responsibilities of the higher post. This policy is usually found in larger organizations where it is possible to return an employee to a lower grade. For example, the police service promotes its sergeants 'on probation' for a year before substantiating their rank. Other organizations use acting and temporary periods of duty before any promotion is considered, but these are only useful if adequate assessments are made by their line managers.

DISMISSAL IN CAPABILITY CASES

If despite attempts to encourage an employee to improve to an acceptable level of performance the employee's work continues to be unsatisfactory, the option of dismissal may be regarded by management as the appropriate, if not inevitable, solution. However, before such a decision is taken the employee should be given a further opportunity to explain why they are not measuring up to the organization's requirements for the job. This explanation should be heard by a member of management who has the authority to take a dismissal decision if they consider it appropriate. But the process of reaching that decision should involve that member of management considering each of the following questions in sequence and being able to answer each with a reasonably confident 'Yes':

1. Has there been as much investigation of the employee's lack of capability and the possible reasons for it, as is reasonable in the circumstances?
2. Have I considered any points put forward by or on behalf of the employee by way of explanation for their inadequate performance at work?
3. Do I genuinely believe that the circumstances render the satisfactory performance of the employee's contract unlikely?
4. Have I reasonable grounds on which to sustain that belief on the balance of probabilities (that is, is it more likely than less likely that the employee's capability will continue to be below an acceptable level)?
5. Are the circumstances, having regard to the employee's job and the interests of the employee's job and the interests of the organization, sufficiently serious in the light of the facts about their capability which I have found to be established to justify the decision I am contemplating?
6. Have I provided the employee or their representative with an opportunity to put forward any points for me to consider in mitigation before deciding whether or not to dismiss, including the offer of alternative employment, and have I had regard to these (and to any response to them by the employee's manager)?
7. Is the decision within the band of reasonable responses of a reasonable employer in the circumstances?

I have included considerable detail in this chapter because I know managers have difficulty in this area. Most advice in the law books focuses on the ways managers could defend a claim after the dismissal. I wanted to set out the tactics to follow to improve an employee's performance, or if this fails, to carry out a dismissal process as free from any risk as possible.

If in the end it is necessary to dismiss an employee for lack of capability, the least the employer must be prepared to do is to show that it had a reasonable ground for believing that the employee was incompetent. In coming to that conclusion and implementing the dismissal decision, the manager must have discussed the employee's weaknesses with them and have acted reasonably, fair and consistently.

The two questions the process needs to address are:

▌ Did the employer honestly and reasonably hold the belief that the employee was not competent?
▌ Was there a reasonable ground for that belief?

The eminent judge Lord Denning said:

> Whenever a man is dismissed for incapacity or incompetence it is sufficient that the employer honestly believes on reasonable grounds that the man is incapable or incompetent. It is not necessary for the employer to prove that he is in fact incapable or incompetent.

CAPABILITY AND DISABILITY

We shall look separately at the topic of disability, but it is important to reinforce the responsibilities at this stage, while we are dealing with capability. Employees have a particular responsibility with regard to disabled persons in that 'a person discriminates against a disabled person if he fails to comply with a duty to make reasonable adjustments imposed on him in relation to the disabled person' (Section 3A(2) Disability Discrimination Act 1995).

7

Special circumstances

INTRODUCTION

There are a range of areas under which an employee could raise a grievance or a complaint resulting in an investigation, discipline investigation
and disciplinary action. Space does not allow a comprehensive explanation
but I want to include sufficient advice to point the manager in the right
direction. When dealing with allegations of discrimination or harassment,
it is important that the investigator understands policies and 'best practice'
basics of the law. The Commission for Equality and Human Rights (CEHR)
is now responsible for the whole area of age, disability, gender, race, religion and sexual orientation and will have a duty to promote and uphold
the Human Rights Act. Its website (www.equalityhumanrights.com/) is a
good source of advice and guidance in these areas.

Many of the grievances raised by employees relate to terms and conditions, the application of specific company policies, like family-friendly
legislation, or the decisions made by management in respect of their
working conditions. These are quite different from the grievances or
complaints that allege misconduct on behalf of others. In larger organizations, this type of 'administrative' grievance will be directed to personnel
or human resources. Many readers will own or work in smaller units

without the benefit of qualified human resources staff. In fact, one of the declared objectives of this book is to be of practical help to this group.

Before embarking on this I would advice managers dealing with complex grievances to recognize when they are out of their depth and need to seek professional advice. For example, I recently dealt with a grievance for a client who had received a complaint from an employee returning to work after additional maternity leave. She had been a part-time employee prior to her confinement. She complained about not being able to return to the same job she had previously held, sex discrimination, unfair treatment as a part-time worker and breach of contract. In this case none of the complaints were justified. However, my point is a small employer could not be expected to deal with this type of grievance without a little help, and could end up in litigation unnecessarily.

The law in these areas is constantly changing. Over recent years the several new areas have been introduced, such as religious belief, part-time employees, age discrimination and third-party harassment.

DEFINITIONS

Grievances or complaints may be submitted alleging harassment, direct or indirect discrimination on any of the grounds listed in this chapter, or that employees have suffered a detriment. While a detailed explanation of discrimination law is outside our scope, a few definitions may help in understanding the basics.

'Harassment' is concerned with unwanted conduct on one of the protected grounds that has the purpose or effect of violating a person's dignity or creating for that person an intimidating, hostile, degrading, humiliating or offensive environment having regard to all the circumstances and the perception of the victim. There is a slightly different definition in respect of sexual harassment, which is unwanted verbal or physical conduct of a sexual nature.

It is important to note that the intention and the motive of the 'harasser' are irrelevant in proving harassment. Examples of harassment include:

- ridicule, embarrassing remarks or jokes, unwelcome comments about dress, appearance, physical or mental impairments;
- deliberate abuse or insults;
- nicknames or name calling;
- graffiti;
- offensive e-mails;

▌ hostile action intended to isolate the victim, unjustifiable criticisms, giving too much or too little work;

▌ unwanted physical contact, demands for sexual favours;

▌ physical assaults.

The term 'detriment' can be defined as when a reasonable worker would or might take the view that the treatment complained of had placed them at a disadvantage in the circumstances in which they had to work. The important aspect is that it is a detriment from the viewpoint of the victim.

'Direct discrimination' is where one worker is treated differently from another because of their race, sex, disability and so on. At the organizational level, examples such as promotion decisions based on race, gender or age are relatively uncommon although they could be alleged in a grievance. Harassment is a more common example of direct discrimination.

'Indirect discrimination' is a more difficult concept and differs slightly in the Race Relations and Sex Discrimination Acts. Generally it is defined as when a requirement, condition or criterion applies equally to all but it places persons of a particular race, sex, disability, age and so on, at particular disadvantage when compared with others.

Managers must be aware that the law gives protection to persons who make complaints under the discrimination legislation by providing that it is unlawful to treat anyone less favourably than another by reason that they have instigated proceedings or done any one of a number of related actions (such as make a complaint to their employer). This is 'victimization'. The wording of this provision is similar in all legislation relating to diversity, including race, ethnicity, gender, marriage or single-sex partnerships, sexual orientation, age, disability, part-time working and so on.

Refusing to deal with a complaint, failing to take appropriate action or subjecting the complainant to any form of detriment will be treated seriously.

BULLYING

Bullying is undoubtedly a problem in the workplace and has been so for many years. As such there may be grievances or complaints in this regard and managers will need to investigate with a view to disciplinary action. Bullying is listed as unacceptable behaviour in all discipline and equality of opportunities policies, and is a real source of stress and disharmony.

However, this type of behaviour is not so clear-cut if it is not based on one of the prohibited areas, such as race, gender and disability. There is no specific offence, for example, of harassment by a white indigenous male on a white indigenous male unless there are issues relating to such areas as sexual orientation or age, and a similar position exists between others when a prohibited area is not in evidence. There is some support in this area from the Protection of Harassment Act 1997 which, although not designed for employment situations, could be used in either criminal or civil court action.

Evidence gathering is notoriously difficult. Bullying seldom takes place in the sight and hearing of others, and if it does, witnesses are often reluctant to get involved. Bullying can be aggressive and oppressive but it can also be extremely subtle such as ignoring victims. There may be allegations of common law or criminal assault, and these should be dealt with as such. Of course, a failure to deal adequately with such an allegation could give the victim reasons to resign and claim constructive unfair dismissal.

It is fair to add that not all relationship difficulties between men and women or employees from different racial groups are discriminatory; some may be simple clashes of personality. But do not forget that the perception of discrimination is sufficient for the matter to need to be explored carefully.

THIRD-PARTY HARASSMENT

It is unlawful for an employer to fail to take reasonably practical steps to protect employees from harassment by third parties where such harassment is known to have occurred on at least two other occasions (Reg. Sex Discrimination Act 1975 (Amendment Regulations 2008)): see Case study 2.

SEX AND RELATED FORMS OF DISCRIMINATION

This area is a source of both grievances and complaints of harassment that will require particular attention. Investigators will need to tread with care in dealing with the complaint and in their evidence gathering. Discrimination on grounds of sex, marital status, pregnancy, sexual orientation, gender reassignment and so on, is often included in general grievances against management decisions. Specific advice is recommended in complex cases. It should not be forgotten that both men and women are protected by the prohibition on sex discrimination under the legislation.

RACE

Grievances and complaints of discrimination on race (including colour, nationality, and ethnic or national origins) or similar grounds are complex, and employers are advised to seek specialist assistance in investigating such matters. Discrimination on grounds of race can also be included in general grievances against management decisions. Again, specific advice is recommended.

DISABILITY

Much of what has been said in other categories applies to grievances or complaints of disability discrimination. A person has a disability for these purposes if they have a physical or mental impairment which has a substantial and long-term adverse effect on their ability to carry out normal day-to-day activities. There are a great many cases illuminating this definition and it can become quite complex. For practical purposes, a relevant permanent condition is included but also a 'temporary' condition that has the specified effects and lasts for over 12 months. In some circumstances, the term 'disability' includes employees who would not see themselves as disabled, nor perhaps would their colleagues or employer: for example those with depression, back problems and temporary health issues.

However, there is an additional concept that employers are obliged to consider with regard to disability. There is a duty on employers to make what the legislation terms 'reasonable adjustments'. These might include altering premises and access, installing or modifying equipment and providing a whole range of support. If grievances are received in these areas careful research will be needed before responding. The resources of the employer are taken into account in assessing what may be a reasonable adjustment, and there is ample guidance and advice available, and occasionally grants to assist with some of the work.

BURDEN OF PROOF IN DISCRIMINATION CASES

There is a particular rule concerning the burden of proof that investigators should bear in mind. The normal standard of proof is the balance of probabilities that discrimination occurred. European directives have introduced the process whereby the burden of proof transfers from the employee to the employer. In essence, where the employee establishes facts from which a tribunal could conclude in the absence of an adequate explanation that the employer committed an unlawful act (of discrimination), the complaint will be upheld unless the employer proves that it did not commit that act. The relevance of this to the employer in a discipline or grievance scenario is that it should accept the complaint on face value and investigate accordingly.

HIV AND AIDS

The Terrence Higgins Trust (www.tht.org.uk) estimates that there are 65,000 people with HIV in the United Kingdom, and probably a third are undiagnosed. HIV is deemed to be a disability and the usual protection applies. As stated there are undiagnosed cases and these place no obligation on an employer. However, there are also those with HIV infection who choose, for what may be very good reasons as seen by themselves, not to inform their employer. If this information gets known in the workplace it has the potential to cause problems with other employees and will need very careful handling. Some of the extremely negative feelings around several years ago are beginning to change as awareness grows of the low level of risk in normal contact. If grievances are received in this subject area you are advised to seek advice and guidance. It is not unknown for workers to refuse to work with HIV sufferers. There is also help and guidance from NHS units.

RELIGIOUS BELIEF

'Religion' or 'belief' is not specifically defined in the regulations (Employment Equality (Religion or Belief) Regulations 2003) and some lawyers suggest it covers fringe religions and religious cults as well as the usual list of mainstream practised religions and beliefs such as Christianity, Islam, Judaism, Buddhism, Rastafarianism, Sikhism, Druidry and Paganism. Direct or indirect discrimination, harassment or victimization on grounds of religion or belief is unlawful. Examples could be refusing employment to members of certain religions (direct) or company rules requiring all security staff to wear peaked caps (indirect to Sikhs). Grievances could be received regarding public holidays, access to areas for prayer and so on. These should be dealt with carefully, and advice and guidance obtained where necessary. In this regard ACAS is always a good starting point.

Some larger organizations have addressed these regulations by allowing believers of other faiths to work on Christian holidays and take a similar number of paid holidays at the time of their religious feasts. This may not be realistic for small employers and this would be recognized.

AGE DISCRIMINATION

Age discrimination entered the law books on 1 October 2006 (The Employment Equality (Age) Regulations 2006) and provides that discrimination or less favourable treatment on the grounds of age, or the perception of age, is illegal. The question of retirement and retirement ages is outside our scope. However, there could well be grievances in this area and an investigation may be necessary.

CRIMINAL OFFENCES – ORGANIZATIONAL OPTIONS

Where the allegation, grievance or the investigation reveals a criminal offence or even the suspicion of such, a decision will be needed on whether the police are to be involved. The decision will be based on the considerations shown in Table 7.1. In an employment context, it was held that an employee's refusal to take part in the employer's investigation does not mean that dismissal, even before the outcome of a criminal trial, would necessarily be unfair (*Harris and anor* v *Courage (Eastern) Ltd* [1981]). It may be reasonable for a lawyer to advice a client not to make any comments while an investigation is taking place. Furthermore, an acquittal in a criminal court would not make a dismissal, based on the same or similar facts, unfair. The standard of proof required is far less onerous.

In practical terms, it may be necessarily to discuss the progress of an internal investigation with police so as not to inhibit or prejudice their work. However, there is no obligation to do so and there is no requirement to report a crime to the police at all.

When faced with a discipline allegation that is or could be criminal, Table 7.1 may help in deciding which course of action to take. In terms of low level crime at work such as theft, minor assaults, possession of drugs, etc, many employers take the disciplinary route, usually resulting in a

Table 7.1 Deciding whether to involve the police

Decision	Advantages	Disadvantages
No further action An unlikely decision!	No cost in money or time May sometimes be the 'right' decision? Could return to 'bite you'	Failure to allay suspicions Clear message that 'staff can get away with it' Possibility of adverse publicity if suspicions become public knowledge Feelings of complainant
Utilization of an appropriate manager from another area	May be required by policy No incremental cost other than time Investigation is controllable	Lack of independence Lack of knowledge of evidence and PACE* and little or no investigatory experience (perhaps) May delay involving police until too late to resolve
HR staff to investigate Is this really their job? I do not think it should be	Familiar with organization Can be controlled Good working knowledge of policies and procedures	Lack of independence Lack of knowledge of evidence and PACE, and maybe, little or no investigatory experience May delay involving police until too late to resolve
External specialist/ consultant/ lawyer etc	Independent Knowledge of rules of evidence, evidence gathering, PACE* with investigatory experience Can advice on dealing with press if necessary Can be controlled to reflect organizational needs	High cost implication Lack of extensive knowledge of organization
Police – only if alleged circumstances indicate a crime	No incremental cost Independent Good knowledge of PACE* and investigations Access to large resources Have extra powers Can assist with media	Potentially, little control once case accepted by police Goals tend to evidence gathering for prosecution/ conviction which may not be in organizational interest Lack of sensibilities to organizational requirements

* Police and Criminal Evidence Act 1984, which covers interviewing offenders and evidence gathering

dismissal rather than involving the police. A police investigation could take many months and even longer before a court hearing.

It is preferable not to have police officers present during any disciplinary interview, particularly if the employee does not consent. The interviews should certainly not be held concurrently. One of the issues that arise in these cases and is generally misunderstood is that in a criminal prosecution it is necessary to prove beyond reasonable doubt that the offence took place and that the suspect was guilty of it. In an employment situation it is sufficient to establish that the employer reasonable believed that the employee committed the misconduct.

If your organization is faced with a complex investigation it would be wise to consider external assistance. Inexperienced investigators can lead an organization into treacherous waters, particularly when dealing with well-represented employees or senior staff.

FAILURE TO COMPLY WITH INSTRUCTIONS

There is an implied clause in the contract of employment that an employee is obliged to comply with reasonable instructions or orders. It follows that an employer could take disciplinary action if there is evidence that the employee did not comply. In most cases it would be misconduct dealt with by an informal warning. However, repeated cases could amount to gross misconduct and could, after the necessary process, result in a dismissal.

Changing an employee's duties, level of responsibilities, working hours and so on, is more complex and a contractual issue. There may be flexibility in the contract. If not, an employer cannot arbitrarily vary a contract without consultation and agreement. There are ways of achieving the changes but an employer would be well advised not to take the disciplinary route. If an employee has a good reason for failing to follow an instruction these should be heard and assessed. If necessary a manager should respond before forcing the employee into submitting a formal grievance.

ALCOHOL AND DRUGS

There are several issues falling into this category. Let us first consider drinking on duty: that is, while being paid to carry out contractual tasks and responsibilities. There is no general and absolute ban; it depends on the circumstances. For example, many employees are allowed to drink at product launches or retirement parties in the firm's time. Although the practice is considerably less than it was in the period from the 1960s to the 1980s, the 'liquid lunch' or a 'pie and pint' still exists in some sectors. On the other hand, drinking while driving or operating machinery is totally unacceptable and no one would see it as less than gross misconduct. It is worth pointing out that drinking alcohol, unless under age or driving on a road, is not illegal, whereas many drugs are.

From an employer's point of view the impact of an employee under the noticeable influence of illegal drugs or prescribed medication can be much the same, although the subsequent action will be different. It is fact that some people taking painkillers for a cold or chronic pain could be less than totally attentive to their work.

Many employees place clauses in the contract of employment or a separate code of conduct relating to the use of alcohol and drugs. For example, a statement used by an NHS trust is:

General Fitness for Work

In order to discharge responsibilities safely, efficiently and effectively, staff are expected to be generally fit for work. Staff must not report for duty under the influence of alcohol, drugs or other substances to the extent that it may affect their own performance or safety, or the safety of others. The consumption of alcohol, or the misuse of drugs or other substances, is not permitted during any period of duty, and staff who are considered under the influence will be suspended immediately in order that the matter can be investigated. It is recognized that some staff do experience personal or medical problems which become associated with the use of alcohol, drugs or other substances. Every effort will be made, with the co-operation of the employee, to provide counselling and support to overcome the difficulties in order to protect the individual's employment. Termination of employment will be considered as a last resort where all attempts to seek co-operation of the employee or to bring about an improvement have failed.

Some may consider this to be overkill, although I think it is very useful. I see it as best practice. Occasionally employment contracts, including some in local authorities, include a clause that alcohol can only be consumed at work with the express permission of a senior manager.

When confronted by these problems, most employers would start the process as one of discipline and I would recommend this. Once the process is under way it is then relatively simple to move to a welfare, counselling, medical or capability procedure. It is extremely difficult to move from adopting a welfare approach and then revert to discipline. Many employers are beginning to take a more enlightened approach to misuse of drugs, but whichever position you take, I urge you to be consistent.

On the point of contracts, some employers insert a clause giving them the right to ask for a blood test when the influence of drink or drugs is suspected. These should only be taken by a medically qualified person and will require the consent of the employee, otherwise it would be considered an assault. The standard of proof in discipline cases would support a dismissal on a suspicion of alcohol or drugs based on reasonable grounds. However, a medical examination would be preferable.

To summarize this section, driving or operating machinery under the influence of alcohol or drugs is clearly gross misconduct and would, in most cases, merit suspension, investigation, discipline hearing, and if established, dismissal. The same would apply to any dealing in illegal drugs in the workplace (a conviction for drug dealing outside work may also warrant disciplinary action). Dependency on these substances may lead an employer to supportive action. This would depend on the size and resources of the organizations, its general activities and the position it takes. I would repeat the need to be consistent in approach to these difficult, but not uncommon, problems.

LOSS OF DRIVING LICENCE

This topic is difficult to place but worthy of inclusion. The loss of a driving licence for drink-driving offences has been with us for some time, in particular after the introduction of the breathalyser in 1965, and today the matter is aggravated by the increase in the number of speed enforcement cameras and the collecting of penalty points leading to a driving ban. Is this a disciplinary issue? One of the potentially fair reasons for dismissal includes the failure to meet a legal requirement for carrying out particular types of employment. If you employ someone as a driver and they lose their driving licence they cannot do their job. This is a fair reason to dismiss but should progress through a formal disciplinary process.

However, employers may wish to take a more considered approach. What is the length of the ban? What was the level of excess alcohol in their blood? What were the circumstances? And probably more importantly, what are the level of resources and employment opportunities within the organization to offer non-driving work during the period of the ban? For example, a firm might find alternative work for a sales person after a three-month ban for several excess speed convictions. A two-year driving ban for causing death by dangerous driving is a different matter. In addition, the resources of the organization are of relevance in this decision.

TRADE UNION REPRESENTATIVES

If it is established that an employee has been dismissed for trade union membership or activity this will be an automatically unfair dismissal regardless of the formality of the decision. It is essential, therefore, that employers take care when instigating disciplinary cases against trade union officials. This is not to say that misconduct by a trade union representative should not be dealt with. It should, but care must be taken. In most cases employers are advised to involve regional officials of the trade union at some stage.

DATA PROTECTION AND HUMAN RIGHTS

The Human Rights Act and the Data Protection Act, both of 1998, have had an impact on employment in the United Kingdom. A discussion of all the issues is beyond our scope here but there are a few elements of relevance to our topic area. Some employers use CCTV, security staff, checking telephone calls (especially to premium charge lines), opening e-mails, checking website visits and so on.

Eight data protection principles

The Data Protection Act 1998 lists eight data protection principles relating to the processing of personal data held on manual or computerized filing systems. Personal data held on an employee's personal file or on any associated or computerized record must comply with the following.

1. Data must have been obtained fairly and lawfully.
2. Data must not be held on file other than for a legitimate purpose (not be used or made use of for any other purpose).
3. Data must be adequate, relevant and not excessive in relation to the purpose or purposes for which it is kept.
4. Data must be accurate and, where necessary, kept up to date.
5. Data must not be kept for longer than is absolutely necessary.
6. Data must be held in compliance with an employee's rights of access to personal data, must not be processed in a way calculated (or likely) to cause damage or distress to an employee, and must be corrected, erased or destroyed if inaccurate or no longer relevant.

7. Data must be protected (by the best available means) against unauthorized access or disclosure and against accidental loss, damage or destruction, and must be treated as confidential by the staff to whom they are entrusted.

8. Data must not be transferred to any country or territory (eg to a parent or controlling company) outside the European Economic Area.

Duties of employers

Personal data must have been obtained by fair and lawful means. It must not be kept on an employee's personal file for longer than is necessary, nor without the employee's express consent (preferably given in writing) unless the data in question is needed to determine an employee's suitability or continued suitability for employment or to facilitate compliance with either party's legal or contractual obligations. This would include certain obligations under the Asylum and Immigration Act, monitoring the health of employees who are, or may be, exposed to prescribed hazardous substances and so on.

As we have seen earlier, employees have an implied contractual duty of fidelity and trust. Employers may retain data or evidence of a breach of that duty (poor attendance, insubordination, misconduct, non-compliance with health and safety rules and so on) and may need to produce it in evidence before an employment tribunal or court to justify its decision to discipline or dismiss such an employee. Attendance records (supported by doctors' sick notes, accident reports and so on) must be maintained for that very same reason, as must records of disciplinary warnings and hearings.

Evidence of an employee's background and educational attainments (supported by performance assessments and progress reports) is also necessary in order to determine present and future training needs or to establish whether or not a particular employee is ready for promotion or transfer. Even details of an employee's home address, telephone number and next of kin should arguably be kept on file for use in the event of an accident or other emergency. The same could be said of the information to be found in the vast array of documents customarily held on an employee's personal file. If they do not serve a useful or legitimate purpose, they should be removed and destroyed.

Many employers will add a clause in the employment contract, or statement of main terms, relating to the processing of personal and sensitive data, and I would recommend the outline in the box as appropriate.

Data protection

You hereby give consent to [the employer] to process data concerning you in order to properly fulfil its functions to you under the contract and for reasons relating to your employment as required by the Data Protection Act 1998 (DPA). We anticipate that such processing will principally relate to personnel, administrative and payroll issues.

As part of such consent you agree that [the employer] may need to process 'sensitive personal data' (as defined by the DPA) in relation to you for its legitimate business needs and you undertake to sign on request any such express consent as may be required to enable [the employer] to do so.

Rights of employees

Any employee who is concerned about the nature, content, accuracy or relevance of the personal data held on a relevant filing system may make a written 'data subject access request'. An employer must provide the required information within 40 days of receiving it.

The Information Commissioner is in post to enforce the data protection laws, and has issued a code of practice. Part 3 (www.ico.urg.uk) deals with monitoring at work. We are living in a world of more and more monitoring and surveillance, and this is evident in the workplace:

Monitoring is a recognized component of the employment relationship. Most employers will make some checks on the quantity and quality of work produced by their workers. Workers will generally expect this. Many employers carry out monitoring to safeguard workers, as well as to protect their own interests or those of their customers. For example, monitoring may take place to ensure that those in hazardous environments are not being put at risk through the adoption of unsafe working practices. Monitoring arrangements may equally be part of the security mechanisms used to protect personal data/personal information. In other cases, for example in the context of some financial services, the employer may be under legal or regulatory obligations which it can only realistically fulfil if it undertakes some monitoring. However where monitoring goes beyond one individual simply watching another and involves the manual recording or any automated processing of personal information, it must be done in a way that is both lawful and fair to workers.

Monitoring may, to varying degrees, have an adverse impact on workers. It may intrude into their private lives, undermine respect for their correspondence or interfere with the relationship of mutual trust and confidence that should exist between them and their employer. The extent to which it does this may not always be immediately obvious. It is not always easy to draw a distinction between work-place and private information. For example monitoring e-mail messages from a worker to an occupational health advisor, or messages between workers and their trade union representatives, can give rise to concern.

The above extract indicates that what the Act requires is that any adverse impact on workers is justified by the benefits to the employer and others. This code is designed to help employers determine when this might be the case. The code goes on to distinguish between systematic and occasional monitoring, with more concern and guidance on the former.

The code lists alternatives or different methods of monitoring, and many of these could be useful in the field of discipline and grievance. Considering alternatives, or different methods of monitoring, means asking questions such as:

- Can established or new methods of supervision, effective training and/or clear communication from managers, rather than electronic or other systemic monitoring, deliver acceptable results?
- Can the investigation of specific incidents or problems be relied on, for example accessing stored e-mails to follow up an allegation of malpractice, rather than undertaking continuous monitoring?
- Can monitoring be limited to workers about whom complaints have been received, or whom there are other grounds to suspect wrongdoing?
- Can monitoring be targeted at areas of highest risk: for example, can it be directed at a few individuals whose jobs mean they pose a particular risk to the business rather than at everyone?
- Can monitoring be automated? If so, will it be less intrusive: for example, it might mean that private information will be 'seen' only by a machine rather than by other workers.
- Can spot-checks or audit be undertaken instead of using continuous monitoring? Remember, though, that continuous automated monitoring could be less intrusive than spot-checks or audits that involve human intervention.

It all rather boils down to making a conscious decision that can be justified in the prevailing circumstances, which might, of course, be an allegation or grievance.

Human Rights Act 1998

Based on the European Convention of Human Rights, this Act does not give employment tribunals the power to hear 'free-standing' complaints under its provisions. It sets a framework under which tribunals, public bodies and others should operate. In our topic area, it includes issues such as:

- the right to a fair trial (this, as principle, includes discipline hearings);
- the right to respect for private and family life (this has been *unsuccessfully* used to challenge the monitoring of employees to see if they are genuinely ill, undertaking other employment or falsifying timesheets (*McGowan* v *Scottish Water* [2005] IRLR 167));
- freedom of thought, conscience and religion (the driving force behind the religious belief regulations);
- a prohibition of discrimination.

As we examine evidence and evidence gathering you may realize that in some discipline investigations it will be necessary to find alternative methods of gathering the evidence needed to prove a case.

MISUSE OF TELEPHONE, E-MAIL OR INTERNET

I have been involved in several cases of discipline and dismissal for internet misuse over the past couple of years. It is definitely on the increase but, as with many forms of misconduct, it is a matter of degree, evidence and the employer's attitude. Some acts are clearly wrong and should be considered misconduct, and in some cases gross misconduct. For example:

- downloading and possibly circulating pornography;
- sending abusive or insulting e-mails to colleagues.
- accessing colleagues' passwords in order to use the system for the above purposes.

These matters could amount to sexual harassment.

Playing computer games and checking holiday availability and train timetables for private journeys are somewhat different.

For many years there have been cases of employees being disciplined for excess use of the firm's telephone for personal calls. This is becoming more of a problem with the advent of premium charges on some numbers and relatively new temptations like voting on television reality programmes.

The key is to draft and circulate a policy and clear rules on the use of telephones (land line and mobiles), the internet in general and private use in particular. These rules should be included in the induction course and included in the checklist to be signed by all employees.

A relatively recent problem in the area of the internet and the world wide web is that of personal blogs and social network sites. Not only are some employees spending an inordinate amount of work time on these pursuits, they could be divulging personal data or confidential information. Employers have every right to monitor this activity under their policy and take action where appropriate.

8

Evidence and evidence gathering

WHAT EVIDENCE IS

In order to resolve an employee's grievance satisfactorily or to prove or disprove a discipline allegation, investigators require more than opinion and rumour – they require evidence. In this chapter, we shall be looking at what evidence is and the level required in employment cases – the standard of proof. Everyone who has watched *Poirot* or *Inspector Morse* will know that a case cannot be solved without *evidence* – speculation, rumour or even 'gut feelings' are insufficient to gain a conviction or justify a dismissal or warning.

At this early stage it will be useful to consider the nature of evidence as this is what the investigator is seeking. While the term 'evidence' is a legal concept it is not out of place in any form of investigatory activity. 'Evidence' can be described as 'information by which facts in issue tend to be proved or disproved'. There is a difference between information and evidence. In an investigation you will amass a great deal of information; the question is how much can be relied upon as evidence of fact. Facts supported by evidence can lead to reliable conclusions and guide decision making in situations when a person's livelihood is at risk. Unsupported information can lead to poor conclusions, bad decisions and leave the organization in a position where it would not be able to defend any legal action by a current or ex-employee.

In gathering evidence, an investigator must take an independent approach and not become focused on supporting a hypothesis when evidence to counter it is presented. Avoid the trap suggested by the cliché 'I've made up my mind so don't confuse me with the facts.'

In investigatory work there is a special type of ongoing preparation and planning. This relates to reviewing the information and facts you already have and deciding on the facts or corroboration you still need to obtain. What are the gaps in your evidence? Is there evidence available to fill these gaps? If so, where is it and who can provide it? If not, how can you get around it? For example, Mary states that there were two £20 notes in the petty cash box when she took out some money to buy postage stamps. Peter was alone in the office when she left. When she returned after lunch and put the change back in the petty cash box she noticed that the two £20 notes were missing. This simple scenario contains some facts and some gaps. A general understanding of evidence is critical in filling these gaps in your case. Principally, did Peter take the £20 notes?

At the beginning of an investigation, the key is often the terms of reference and the details of the allegation(s) against an employee. You must always maintain a clear focus on your purpose, which is to find evidence to support the allegation or to disprove it, and above all, to discover the truth. In the case of a grievance investigation the issue complained of should suggest the areas that need to be checked for facts supported by evidence.

The law and procedure relating to evidence is complex, and primarily intended for criminal and civil courts, but the basic principles do apply to discipline cases. You are encouraged to adopt best practice in the gathering and presentation of evidence, primarily in order to fulfil your obligation to be reasonable, fair and consistent. An understanding of the types of evidence will be useful in planning your investigation and directing your activities.

DIRECT EVIDENCE

Direct evidence is the main type of evidence that will enable the investigator to establish facts. Initially, it is evidence that a witness perceives by their senses: something they saw or overheard, something they can give written or verbal testimony about. They were there when the action took place, they saw someone do something, or they heard someone say something. This is evidence from a witness who will, if necessary, tell a discipline hearing what they did, saw or heard. It also includes other 'real' evidence such as original documents, electronic files and CCTV recordings.

Of course, the fact that a witness gives testimony does not, by itself, mean that it is true. Another witness could, and often does, give an entirely different version of the facts. This may be due to good old-fashion lying but it could be their perception of the situation – their perspective of incidents that were not clear. To illustrate this point, imagine that you are in the middle of the road after a football match and watching supporters coming out of one gate wearing red scarves and others emerging from another gate wearing blue scarves. You hear on the radio that the final score was 2–2, as a result of a penalty goal late in the game. If you approached people supporting the 'home' red team do you think you would get the same description of the game as you would from the 'away' blue supporters? I think not! Even without conscious lying, their perceptions would differ.

You, as the investigator, will need to find supporting evidence or corroboration to clarify a situation if there is doubt. There is a danger in assuming additional facts, conclusions or subsequent incidents from known facts. These also need to be proven.

Examples of simple direct evidence from a witness are:

'I saw John take the money out of the till.' However, if John had legitimate access to the till, how far does this evidence take you?

'I saw that Mary was driving the car when it left the yard and that she was alone.' This statement only proves she was driving at that time!

'I was present and heard Peter call Andrew a "gay-boy".'

'I was in the workshop from 9.00 am to 12 noon and Susan did not come in at all.'

'When I returned to the office at 2.00 pm I noticed Mary was crying.' This does not go any way towards establishing why she was crying.

'When I turned on my computer I received the e-mail from George with the indecent image as an attachment.' This may suggest George sent it but it does not conclusively prove that to be the case; someone else could have logged on using his password.

At this stage you should remember that there is a great difference between making a reasonable inference from known facts and making a guess.

CORROBORATION

I used the word corroboration; I ought to explain what it means. This is the legal term for independent evidence which supports other evidence the investigator gathers and implicates the person against whom the allegation has been made. While it is required in some criminal offences it is not necessary in discipline cases. However, if independent testimony can be obtained it is powerful in support of your case.

There are laws and case decisions dictating when corroborating evidence is necessary in criminal cases. An example when this could be required in a discipline case when an employee is found to have been stealing goods. In a statement the employee alleges another worker was also stealing. As an employer or investigator, I would want additional evidence to support this allegation. This is based on the criminal maxim that evidence of an accomplice must be corroborated.

CIRCUMSTANTIAL OR INDIRECT EVIDENCE

Investigators should be aware of circumstantial evidence and its use in discipline cases. Circumstantial evidence is evidence of relevant facts from which the facts in issue may be presumed with more or less certainty, and a reasonable belief may be sufficient. It can be useful when direct evidence is not available. This type of evidence often fulfils the standard of proof necessary in discipline situations. For example, 'When I turned on my computer I received the e-mail from George with the indecent image as an attachment. At the same time I could see through the glass partition that George was sitting at his computer.' This is not direct evidence that George sent the indecent image but it would support such an inference. The matter could be totally satisfied by technical evidence, maybe from your IT specialist, to the effect that an e-mail message including the attachment was from George and it could only have been sent from his computer terminal.

Take another example: a factory security log records a sales person taking a certain vehicle out of the car park at 10.00 am and returning at 4.00 pm. It could be presumed, in the absence of evidence to the contrary, that this person was in charge of the vehicle when it was damaged at 1.00 pm.

ADMISSIBILITY AND WEIGHT

There are two legal concepts that need to be applied to evidence: 'admissibility' and 'weight'. The former – whether evidence is to be allowed – is not a real problem in the employment situation, as the decision whether or not a particular piece of evidence is allowed is one for the discipline panel chair. The investigator should include all the available evidence in their report, for example, a witness statement made by an employee who had subsequently been dismissed for gross misconduct and falsehood in another matter. In order to be fair, this may or may not be allowed by the discipline hearing.

The decision what weight to attach to a particular piece of evidence is crucial, and needs to be addressed in the report. Some evidence is more reliable than other evidence. This may be a factor relating to the reliability of the witness, their physical positioning relative to the incident in question, their involvement in the incident, their relationship to others – but not, of course, their seniority or grade.

OPINIONS

Unless someone is a recognized expert such as a doctor, or health and safety expert, their opinion is usually given less weight than the facts of what they actually heard or saw. A discipline hearing or grievance hearing may seek opinion or expert evidence to describe the legal position, technical details, accountancy practices and so on. Some opinions – what people think – are totally useless and take the investigation no further forward. For example, 'I don't know why but I always thought John was racist.' 'I never did trust Mary from accounts.'

HEARSAY EVIDENCE

This is evidence of something a person does not know for themselves but has been told by another. However, statements made by others in the sight and hearing of the suspect are not hearsay because that person has had the opportunity to comment, and maybe deny them. Hearsay is not totally reliable and should be avoided if possible.

In employment cases, discipline panels may find that they form a reasonable opinion of guilt or innocence based on some level of indirect or hearsay evidence. This would not normally be possible in criminal or civil cases.

EARLY COMPLAINT IN CASES OF SEXUAL HARASSMENT

One special category of hearsay evidence is allowed in criminal law, and I see no reason why it should not be used in employment cases when available. This is called 'early complaint'. When a woman is sexually harassed or even subject to sexual assault within the workplace, she may not make a formal complaint at that stage but she may confide in a workmate. If the matter does result in a discipline investigation, possibly much later, the evidence of the 'confidant' could be used although it is hearsay: that is, not said in the presence of the suspect. It helps to get around the fact that where sexual harassment occurs it is often not within the sight and hearing of potential witnesses.

DOCUMENTARY EVIDENCE

This form of evidence often features in discipline cases. A document could be a report, statement, letter, timesheet, standard operating procedure or policy. Also, in this context, the word 'document' includes maps, plans, graphs, checklist, drawings, photographs, discs, tapes, video tapes and films.

To be accepted without argument, a document should be the original. A copy (secondary evidence) may be accepted but could give rise to a dispute over its accuracy and authenticity. Evidence often includes documents, although in some cases these are given less weight than other sources. For example, organizational documents such as timesheets may be contradicted by witness evidence.

An investigator should ensure that as soon as documentary evidence is found it is seized and isolated until the hearing, if this is at all possible.

THE 'BEST EVIDENCE' RULE

This is another criminal concept but very useful in discipline investigations when planning your evidence gathering. The best evidence of a particular fact or facts is provided by the actual complainant, the direct witness or the original document. The rule requires that only the people having immediate personal knowledge of a fact in issue give evidence. A fact in issue means one of the 'points to prove' to establish the case. Any copy or secondary evidence is less convincing and could raise a challenge why the 'best evidence' was not used.

THE BURDEN OF PROOF

While this book is not about tactics in employment tribunals or other courts, some of the ideas from this arena are valid. In cases of discipline the burden or onus is on those bringing an allegation to prove it.

Employees should not be required to prove their innocence unless and until a case is established against them; this will be self-evident in some cases but much more complex in others. For example, in simple cases of lateness or failure to submit a report on time, evidence from the manager that the employee was not where they should be or the report was not received should be enough to require the employee to make an admission or present some valid reason for their behaviour. More complex issues such as, for example, falsifying expenses or bullying would require a body of evidence from both witnesses and IT/paper records. We shall explain how to do this later.

It follows therefore that in many discipline cases, an investigator needs to clarify the points to prove and seek out relevant evidence before presenting a case for discipline.

If an investigator is inexperienced, careless or takes things for granted, an acceptable case before a disciplinary hearing may not be made. In this case it is open to the employee charged with the offence to invite the chair or panel to dismiss the matter before attempting to defend themselves. This would, of course, leave the manager or investigator bringing the case in a very poor light.

The investigation of grievances can be a little different. Some grievances end up with a discipline investigation against an employee while others are complaints against policy, administration or management decisions.

BURDEN OF PROOF IN DISCRIMINATION CASES

There are a special set of rules to meet European requirements in respect of unlawful discrimination. These are of significance in court proceedings but should not be ignored when conducting investigations or dealing with grievances in this area. It should be remembered that allegations of discrimination could be against individuals and/or the company, and in the former case, the employer could be held liable for discrimination by an employee.

The burden of proof is in two stages. First, the person making the allegation – the victim – must provide facts to demonstrate that (in the absence of a satisfactory explanation) a possible case of discrimination has taken place and there has been less favourable treatment. Second, and following on from this, the person against whom the allegation is made (or the employer) must show that the act was not unlawful (*Igen* v *Wong* [2003] IRLR 258, CA). These are complex legal concepts but the investigator looking into these areas should be experienced and knowledgeable, even in the internal grievance or discipline situation. It follows, therefore, that any investigation into alleged discrimination or harassment needs to be detailed and take in all the relevant circumstances, history, policies and personalities.

THE STANDARD OF PROOF

In criminal hearings, evidence must be presented to establish facts and prove a case beyond reasonable doubt. A jury must believe the evidence so as to be sure of the guilt of the accused person. This is the highest level of proof and subject to close scrutiny by judges. In civil courts the standard is one of a balance of probabilities – 'is one scenario more likely than another?' A court must be satisfied that it is more likely than not (or more probable than not) that the relevant fact is established (*R* v *Swaysland* [1987]).

In employment-related cases, including discipline within an organization, the standard is similar. The standard is one of 'reasonableness'. In determining the reasonableness of an employer's decision to dismiss, a tribunal may only take account of those facts (or beliefs) that were known to the employer at the time of the dismissal. Generally speaking, a dismissal will not be made reasonable after the dismissal takes place, nor made unreasonable or unfair by evidence that comes to notice after the dismissal (*W Devis and Sons Ltd* v *Atkins* [1977]). The standard was affirmed by the Court of Appeal (*Foley* v *Post Office* and *HSBC Bank Plc* v *Madden* [2000]) in considering whether, in the particular circumstances of each case, the decision to dismiss fell within a band of reasonable responses which a reasonable employer might have adopted.

As guidance to those conducting discipline investigations and chairing discipline panels, the Burchell test has been established and upheld by the courts (*British Home Stores* v *Burchell* [1980]). The evidence adduced in the investigation must be sufficient for the disciplinary panel to believe that:

- the employer had a genuine belief that the employee was guilty of misconduct;
- the employer had in its mind reasonable grounds upon which to sustain that belief;
- at the stage at which the employer formed that belief on those grounds, there had been as much investigation into the matter as was reasonable in the circumstances.

This means that the employer need not have conclusive direct proof of the employee's misconduct, only a genuine and reasonable belief, reasonably tested.

The role of the employee and their adviser in any subsequent discipline hearing is not to prove innocence, although that would be fatal to your case, but to cast a reasonable doubt on the reasonable belief of guilt the panel might have.

As a prime aim of this book is to avoid litigation or be in a strong position to defend a claim, this standard of proof should guide the investigator in discipline cases.

PRESUMPTIONS

There is a body of law relating to presumptions. Bearing in mind the standard of proof in discipline matters, an investigator may invite a disciplinary panel to make certain presumptions without the necessity to provide evidence. For example, it can be presumed that an experienced operator knows the standard operating procedures for their area of work.

IT EVIDENCE

The use of computers, hand-held devices, mobile telephones and so on, means that a great deal of evidence that used to be in document form is now in an electronic form. This does not change the rules but does have an impact on security and presentation. Just as documents can be destroyed and altered, so can electronic data. Most IT technicians employed within organizations will have the skill and software to recover files and images deleted from a storage device, hard disk, memory stick and so on. In addition, these technicians should be able to tell you when a file was created, saved and amended, and perhaps by whom.

However, if a storage device has been wiped clean by reformatting, the data is usually irrecoverable. In the event of serious issues like high-value financial irregularities or downloaded pornographic images, the police and some financial organizations have software that can recover files from this state.

HOW TO GATHER EVIDENCE

Each case an investigator is charged to substantiate will have certain elements that form the 'points to prove'. It will be necessary to obtain evidence, or an admission, to prove each point. The necessary points to prove are listed for each of the case studies at the end of the book, and suggestions made for how each one could be established.

Some evidence will be obvious. Some may be even given to you when you begin to investigate, such as a statement of complaint, an allegation or a grievance. Sometimes the evidence, or more likely the allegation, is confused and contradictory. Yet even, on some occasions, the initial allegation may be totally false. This is the challenge to the investigator. In some cases you may be asked to investigate a matter for which there is no suspect, for example money or property missing from the locker room.

Evidence gathering and ascertaining the truth, which may of course involve disproving an allegation, is the test of a good investigator. Collecting relevant interview notes and statements, documentary evidence, and using them to prove or disprove a case of misconduct is an interesting but serious business. Furthermore, it will take an employee or manager into areas about which they may have little knowledge or experience. The following chapters will help in your task and in developing the skills necessary to be successful.

In gathering together evidence for a discipline investigation, sometimes known as 'getting all your ducks in a row', you will need to be like the mother duck – organized, persistent and thorough.

DRAFTING A CHRONOLOGY

Reading a report, a series of witness statements or understanding a complex set of circumstances can be difficult, and often involves moving back and forward through a file. Many investigators resolve this by drafting a chronology, a table of effects, meetings, incidents, letters and so on, set out in a timeframe from the earliest relevant event to the latest. The table should include names, cross-references to evidence and links to other key incidents. Chronologies are often prepared as part of the report-writing stage or prior to a hearing.

The reason this tactic has been included at the investigative stage as opposed to the report-writing stage is that it is much better to use a chronology as a dynamic tool. I would advise you to prepare the chronology as soon as you have two or three relevant facts or dates; it should be one of your first steps, not your last. Whenever a witness or item of evidence includes a date or time, you should add it plus a brief note into your chronology. Using a spreadsheet allows you to update and develop your chronology as the investigation progresses. In addition, it is extremely useful to carry your chronology as an aide-memoire when interviewing a witness or reviewing your progress. An example of a chronology is given in Table 8.1.

Table 8.1   A sample investigatory chronology

Discipline Investigation – John Smith – Westfield District Council			
Chronology			
Date	Event	Comments	Reference
14 April 2004	John Smith joined Westfield District Council as an accountant	Qualifications verified	
14 April 2004	John Smith issued with job description	Items 13 Responsibility for ordering stationery and office supplies for council staff and offices	Doc no 2
22 November 2004	John Smith signed for a copy of the revised Westfield District Council Staff Code of Conduct July 2000		Doc no 3
09 April 2006	Mary Smith set up in business, with others, to supply office stationery and similar equipment throughout Westfield District Council	Trading as Acme Office Supplies – Mary Smith is wife of John Smith	
23 May 2006	Publicity material from Acme Office Supplies received by the Council	Passed by reception to John Smith in accordance with standard practice	Doc no 4
29 July 2006	Council Order 1234/06 from John Smith to ABC Stationery Ltd, supplies for past three years		Doc no 5
07 August 2006	e-mail from June Clarke asking John Smith why the stationery order was around 50% of the normal volumes		Doc no 6
25 August 2006	e-mail from June Clarke asking John Smith if he was in a position to reply to her e-mail of 7th August		Doc no 7

Table 8.1 continued

Discipline Investigation – John Smith – Westfield District Council			
Chronology			
Date	Event	Comments	Reference
05 September 2006	e-mail from John Smith to ABC Stationery informing them that the stationery order was low because of the summer holidays and less used		Doc no 8
06 September 2006	John Smith places a substantial stationery order with Acme Office Supplies		Doc no 9
20 September 2006	Stationery order received from Acme Office Supplies and distributed throughout offices		
01 October 2001	Letter from John Smith to ABC Stationery Ltd cancelling the arrangement with the Council	Letter states Council has found more competitively priced alternative	Doc no 10
05 October 2006	Telephone call from Sue Slater, Personnel, complaining of inferior copier paper	see Sue Slater's statement	Statement 2
10 October 2006	John Smith asks George Smithurst to obtain copies of all the Council document copier contracts	see George Smithurst's statement	Statement 3
11 October 2006	John Smith presents a second stationery order to Acme Office Supplies		Doc no 11
23 October 2006	DATE UNCERTAIN – Peter Purvis, Rates office, complains by e-mail to John Smith that suspension files are the wrong size	See Peter Purvis' statement	Doc no 12
02 November 2006	Meeting between Cllr Jones and Council Chief Executive on the subject of a complaint of favouritism to Acme Office Suppliers	Complaint emanated from MD of ABC Stationery Ltd	
04 November 2006	Personnel produced suspension letter on request of CE		Doc no 13
05 November 2006	John Smith formally suspended on full pay by head of personnel		
05 November 2006	Simon Painter, Planning Dept Manager, appointed as investigating officer		

When you do reach the report writing stage it may be necessary to rationalize your chronology to a single page showing key points. Do not forget to retain the original; it will be useful. It is also useful to save all previous versions – they show how the case progressed.

9

The investigation and the investigator

THE INVESTIGATION

An investigation could range from a simple check of a 'signing-in' book to a complex case involved many witnesses, hundreds of papers or electronic documents and lasting several months. The objective of any investigation is to discover the truth and establish the facts. This can only be accomplished by gathering evidence. This chapter, together with Chapter 10 on interviewing, sets out advice and guidance on how to find and assess the evidence.

The intention is not only to build a case against any person(s); it should also be to ascertain the truth as far as is possible. Only when you have the truth, and it is supported by credible evidence, can you begin to prove, or if appropriate disprove, the allegations against the person who is the subject of any allegation. Only when you have the truth can you move from an allegation, maybe in the form of a grievance, to present a case to a disciplinary hearing.

You will remember that the burden and standard of proof does not require an employer to have facts established beyond reasonable doubt. The employer can take action, including a dismissal, on a reasonable belief. However, a good investigator is advised to aim for the best possible level of proof available, and if facts can be proven by weight of evidence that renders them beyond reasonable doubt, so much the better. In the end this can only make the process fair to both the complainant and the person under investigation. As a bonus it makes the task of defending any subsequent claim much easier. Whether it is as part of a discipline allegation or a grievance unrelated to discipline, the good investigator should direct their attentions towards this.

An investigation should be carried out without delay. Fairness and thoroughness are the most important aspects. Wherever possible, the investigator should keep the member of staff informed of the progress. It is unlikely that any recommended timescales in a discipline policy would serve to prevent disciplinary action being taken if the evidence is available. If an employee is represented it would be usual and common courtesy to keep them 'in the loop' on progress and any unforeseen delays.

The instances in which an investigation is undertaken or commenced in secret, that is without the knowledge of the person under investigation, are very limited:

- The issues involved are personally or commercially sensitive.
- Occasionally the police are involved in a wider investigation and request that internal disciplinary action should be suspended. I have known this type of request to be made in cases of drug dealing, organized theft or large-scale fraud.
- In the early stages the identity of the employee(s) involved may be unknown: for example, when investigating missing money or other property.
- There is substantial reason to conduct the investigation in secret: for example, there is a possibility that evidence may be removed or tampered with.
- The suspect should be informed as soon as the reason for secrecy no longer applies.

If the investigation is serious and could involve a dismissal, an investigator may become aware of other people operating in the same area, speaking to the same people and so on. These could be the friends or colleagues of the person under investigation. Natural justice dictates that an 'accused person' should be accorded the opportunity to research matters for their defence, but this should not be allowed to influence, interfere with or prejudice the investigation on behalf of the employer. I recall an investigation into an allegation of racial harassment in a small manufacturing plant where friends of the manager under investigation were attempting to influence Asian workers by threatening their job security. In fact, to a certain extent, the efforts were successful in that some witnesses changed their statements. Investigators should be aware of these problems and ensure their efforts are not obstructed by others.

All of an investigator's activities and progress should be logged at every stage. Nothing should be taken for granted in the early stages and no one involved has the automatic right to be believed.

THE INVESTIGATOR

It is desirable that an investigation is conducted by a manager outside the line management of the worker involved. A complex investigation will require someone who is experienced in this area of work, and it may be necessary to use an external consultant who should be able to offer both the experience and the independence. It is important that investigations are held in confidence and carried out promptly, discreetly and with sensitivity.

Smaller organizations do not have the resources to follow this best practice, and the line manager, investigator and discipline panel chair are sometimes one and the same person. This can even include the task of adjudicating on any appeal. It is fair to say the law does recognize this problem and makes allowances.

USING INTERNAL MANAGERS

Most organizations use internal managers to carry out discipline or grievance investigations. Experience suggests that this is an unpopular duty. An investigation places such managers in unfamiliar situations, leaves them outside their 'comfort zone' and exposes them to scrutiny from a different perspective. Smaller organizations have little choice, of course. A few large organizations, especially in the public sector, have a special team to deal with discipline and complaints: for example police forces, accountants and the medical profession.

My aim is to provide assistance in this important area with sufficient detail and guidance to enable managers to tackle investigations with a degree of confidence. As experience grows, supported by reflective practice, a manager should be able to tackle investigations in a professional and effective manner.

Obviously the grade or level of an investigator needs to be appropriate. The investigator should be at least one grade above the employee under investigation. Care should be taken to select an appropriate investigator for sensitive allegations such as sexual or racial harassment. Some investigations may require specialist skills such as accountancy knowledge when dealing with allegations of fraud within an accountancy unit, an understanding of the law and practice relating to discrimination when dealing with this type of allegation, or IT skills when addressing misuse of software or technical equipment. This can be resolved by using a specialist as an assistant. In cases of discrimination, an investigator of a different gender or race to a complainant may find it beneficial to use an assistant of the same race or gender. This may be essential if there are language difficulties.

EXTERNAL INVESTIGATORS

There are a range of organizations offering experienced investigators, ranging from ex-police or military officers, working in small groups or individually, to highly sophisticated private investigation agencies. Many sector representative bodies maintain lists of ex-senior managers who take on investigations in, for example, local and central government, colleges and universities. Some sectors have their own investigation units while others use the services of auditors and their associated fraud investigation departments. The quality of the external investigator varies enormously. Many are excellent, most are good but some are poor and could leave your organization in a worse position than when the investigation started. A poor investigation could leave an employer exposed to the risk of an employment tribunal claim.

If you do decide to use an external investigator, ensure they are experienced in the area under investigation, for example in fraud, purchasing and supplies, or particularly in discrimination cases.

Obviously minor discipline is better dealt with internally, and large-scale fraud is much better dealt with by professional and specifically experienced investigators. However, in between these extremes there are a wide range of issues – fiddling expenses, sexual harassment, drunkenness, pilfering, bullying, health and safety contraventions and so on – that could be dealt with by the employer or a manager, but not the direct line manager unless there is no alternative. Cost is a factor: investigations can be expensive, and in some cases prolonged.

THE INVESTIGATOR'S SKILL SET

You need to ensure your chosen investigator has the skills to carry out the task. A professional investigator should be experienced but you would be well advised to interview the investigator before agreeing to engage them. Some people just do not fit in, in some organizations. I recall an investigation into corruption involving the supply of materials to a large building site, where the suspects were a director and the site foreman. An auditor was appointed to investigate, and had great difficulties in gathering evidence in an environment so alien to his normal surroundings.

If you are to use internal managers, and discipline investigation is a good way to develop their overall skills, the Table 9.1 checklist may help. Most of the competences listed are self-explanatory but some of the key ones will benefit from an explanation. In particular I have found some to be of great benefit in planning, conducting, reporting on and learning from a wide range of investigations over many years.

REFLECTIVE PRACTICE

This is one of the most important skills linked into continuous development in any managerial activity. Reflective practice is based on David Kolb's learning cycle (Kolb, 1984), and sets out practical steps to learn and develop:

1. The first stage is **concrete experience** – actual experience of a particular event. It could be interviewing a witness or suspect, meeting a 'wall of silence', interviewing a suspect when they are accompanied by an experienced trade union official, presenting evidence to a discipline hearing and so on.
2. The second stage is **reflective observation,** reflecting on the experience and what happened. This is simply thinking about the process in a constructive manner. If you had an assistant or note taker you can use their reflections. Ask yourself pertinent questions such as, Who? What? Where? When? Why? And How? Analyse what happened. How was it different from what you expected? Most importantly, how do you *feel* about the experience?
3. In the third stage move to **abstract conclusion** by drawing conclusions or learning from the experience. For example, concluding that there may be better ways of dealing with a reticent or obstructive witness. What are these alternative ways? What have you learnt? Could you have done better? Did you achieve all or even some of your objectives? Did any of your skills let you down? At the end of this stage decide what to do differently next time.
4. Finally, **active experimentation**, testing or applying your conclusions and new learning on the next opportunity. This should be done during an investigation and at the end of an investigation. Try out

Table 9.1 Checklist of competencies for an investigator

Honesty and Integrity	An investigator needs to instil confidence and resist any pressure to cut corners or act unfairly. If a case results in a dismissal and a claim is made, the quality of the investigation could be an issue under scrutiny.
Ability to work independently	Conducting an investigation can be a lonely business. Few managers are happy to have a colleague 'ferreting around in their area of responsibility'. In cases such as fraud, harassment or bullying, the manager in charge may well be subject to criticism or even discipline.
Logical approach to work	Investigations can only ever be successful if undertaken in a logical manner.
Planning and time management skills	The course of the investigation needs to be planned. Many company policies set out timescales for investigations. It is not uncommon for investigators to have their own management area to take care of while undertaking the enquiry.
Patience and perseverance	Investigations can have blind alleys to retreat from, red herrings to throw back and people, for a variety of reasons, who see it their duty to obstruct your work.
Self-confidence and determination	An investigator cannot be easily distracted and must not take a setback personally.
Problem-solving skills	Having logical processes and tactics to resolve the problems and challenges that face an investigator in a difficult case.
Communication skills	This is a critical area both orally and in writing.
Ability to communicate at all levels	Evidence gathering may require an investigator to speak to potential witnesses at all levels.
Observational skills	A difficult skill to assess but very useful in an investigator.
Body language skills	An appreciation of body language is not just a question of 'reading' someone being interviewed, but also the language demonstrated by the interviewer or investigator.
IT skills	These are needed to record data and produce reports but also to enable an investigator to trace e-mails, etc.
Interviewing skills	A critical skill dealt with in some detail later.
Report writing	You may be surprised that some managers do not need to produce reports in their normal duties, and the skills may not be as widely available as you think.
Reflective practitioner	The ability to review one's own performance and learn from the process.

new ways of doing things, new techniques and so on. In fact, it is quite common to have to change your approach in the middle of an investigation, particularly if you are working in an unfamiliar area.

5.   Then back to **concrete experience** and round the cycle time after time.

There can be no better endorsement than simply to state that this technique works over and over again.

BODY LANGUAGE

This is a natural skill to some, a difficult one to others, and unfortunately a 'dark art' to the rest. However, the skill can be improved upon by awareness, effective training and practice. The only comments I would make here are that body language is a two-way process and it speaks louder than words. While you look at the body language being given out by the person you are interviewing, for example, do not forget that you are emitting body language signals. Try to demonstrate openness and sincerity. You must give the impression you are fair and trustworthy. Avoid being superior, aggressive or 'clever'. Try to give the impression that you are only looking for the truth, which in fact you are.

Look for signs of discomfort, excessive movement, sweating, swallowing and so on. Look for congruence or incongruence between what a witness is saying in answer to your questions and the body language signals they are emitting. People are often quite skilled at making 'their mouths say almost anything' but less so in their body language.

TIME MANAGEMENT

This is a key skill as the pressures on an investigator can be immense. The task may have a preset timescale, you may still have your own section or department to run, and the person who is the subject of the investigation, the suspect's representative and even the complainant will be imposing subtle pressure to get the job finalized or attempting delaying tactics. I find the regular requests for updates from the senior manager nominated to chair any discipline hearing to be irksome. An investigation takes a great deal of organization and discipline. There are three areas that should help you to effectively managing your time.

Self-organization

The *recognition of the need* to develop your time management skills is essential to any real progress. Without this you will not see an actual or potential problems or challenges before they hit your desk, and will have little or no incentive to take remedial action. Effective time management is a change of attitude, and that can only come from inside.

It involves *finding out about 'you'*. This can be achieving by reflective practice, developing self-awareness, seeking feedback (from colleagues and so on) and analysing information; ask yourself 'Where did the time go?'

It involves *setting goals* – personal and professional. It involves drafting and progressing time-based actions plans and even simple daily 'to-do' lists.

Forward planning and priority setting

This is the standard element of time management and critical in any investigation. It involves understanding the difference between 'importance' and 'urgency'. It involves identifying and working to 'must dos', 'should dos' and 'could dos'. Something important is a task or process that is critical to the investigation, something that must be done. Urgent simply means something that must be done by a certain time. Importance and urgency may both apply to a certain task but this is not always the case. For example, it may be important that you return certain files to the finance office, but is it urgent? No.

Priority setting very much encompasses the concepts of undertaking 'progress tasks' in addition to 'maintenance tasks'. Progress tasks are those that move you forward as opposed to maintenance tasks that maintain the status quo.

This skill is particularly important if you are an investigator with your own department or section run in parallel.

Managing relationships and communication

The third, and vitally important, aspect is to *develop the skills to manage your relationships* with your time in mind. It is important to realize and use effective communication techniques and develop strategies to overcome barriers to good communications. You need to develop a range of effective interpersonal skills such as assertiveness, conflict resolution, questioning, listening and building rapport. The critical skill of delegation is also involved. Any appointment to undertake an investigation will take you from your 'day job' and you will need to pass on some of your duties to others.

PROBLEM-SOLVING CHECKLIST

An investigator will inevitably face problems while conducting an investigation. There will be difficult people to deal with, problems in finding ways of establishing a particular fact or tracing the source of certain information, persuading a reluctant witness to cooperate and so on. When normal thought processes do not come up with a solution or strategy, try the discipline of a formal problem-solving cycle. For example:

Identify the problem

What is the issue? Who or what brought it to notice? Are you sure that the stimulus is the real problem and not just a symptom?

1. **Devise your objective(s)** – what is your ideal or realistic outcome? What needs to take place in order to overcome the problem as perceived?
2. **What are the constraints?** What policy, practical, financial, political or inter-personal constraints have an impact on the situation. You cannot do everything – what are the barriers?
3. **Identify options/alternative strategies.** Use a variety of methods to identify a range of solutions. One option to consider is always to take no action – unlikely, but it should not be ignored. Mind-maps may help here: see later. Remember to suspend judgement of the options until this stage is complete.
4. **Evaluate feasible strategies/options.** This is the stage when judgement is reimposed. Some ideas from this stage will be easy to discount; others will need a full cost/benefit analysis, examination of advantages and disadvantages and so on.
5. **Make the decision.** Decide what option or range of options you intend to use. This is the stage to be decisive.
6. **Devise your plan for implementation.** How are you going to put your chosen plan in action? What is to be your strategy?
7. **Communicate to those involved.** Ensure that everyone affected by the problem/solution is aware of the *strategy*, even those not involved in decision.

8. **Build in review stages** – to check that the plan is being implemented as intended. Minor changes can be made if necessary.
9. **Evaluate** – both the process and the outcome. The crucial evaluation is against the objectives you set in stage 2. Do not miss the opportunity to learn from the experience – especially if it was successful!
10. **Revert back** – if necessary, to the initial problem identification, if your plan does not seem to be working. There could be one of several issues: you may have got the problem wrong, the situation/environment may have changed, the process of problem solving may have prompted those involved to mend their ways. You might not have communicated your strategy effectively.

Again, I am happy to declare my commitment to this process when a solution does not readily present itself.

MIND-MAPPING

Mind-maps are the graphical representation of ideas around a central theme. For many, including myself, they are essential in planning an investigation, a report, a discipline hearing presentation, among many other areas, including this book, a holiday and a garden! There are a great many books on the subject, in particular _The Mind-Map Book_ by Tony Buzan (1993). As opposed to conventional notes, mind-maps are dynamic representations of ideas, direct and indirect linkages, and enable the mind to grasp possible relationships between the mass of random facts that can face an investigator in the early stages of an investigation (see page 153).

THE TERMS OF REFERENCE

If an employer is asking a manager or an external investigator to conduct an investigation it will need to ensure that there are adequate and specific terms of reference. In many cases the employee will have been served, whether suspended or not, with details of the allegations against them. These should form the basis of the terms of reference. There may be occasions when the issue to be investigated does not, at the stage of commencing the investigation, have a suspect: for example, missing goods from company stores, anonymous abusive messages sent to a female employee or customer details being passed to a competitor. In addition, a request for a manager to conduct an investigation into an employee's grievance might not be focused on one individual, it might be the application of a company policy.

There may also be a few occasions when the 'suspect' is known but it is decided that the investigation should be keep secret for a while: for example, while evidence is safely obtained or a witness might be at risk. In these cases the employee should be informed of the allegations against them as soon as the reason for secrecy no longer applies.

In addition, a decision will need to be made as to whether the terms of reference are to be expansive, wide or open, as opposed to restricted or closed.

The investigation could be given scope to look into any relevant issues surrounding the allegations or to include any other employee, or group who may be implicated. Alternatively, the terms of reference could limit the investigation specifically to the allegation and the named employee. In most cases the terms of reference will restrict the investigation into the allegations. Any decision to engage in a wider review of a section, process or series of incidents will be left until after any hearing.

TOOLS OF THE INVESTIGATOR

There are a range of tools, techniques and tactics that can further assist an investigator. Of course, experienced practitioners develop their own style and methods of working. The minimum toolkit must contain:

- knowledge of relevant law, policy and procedures;
- planning and time-management skills;
- general interpersonal skills;
- patience and attention to detail;
- interviewing and report-writing skills.

From an employer's point of view, deploying a junior manager to tasks such as investigating discipline or a grievance is an excellent way of developing skills outside their normal professional arena.

USING YOUR CHRONOLOGY

As the investigation develops and our chronology expands, I want to explore a little more of its use. When investigators find themselves at a crossroads or diverted up a blind alley, it is helpful to retrace their steps and start from a known point again; a version of the chronology and indeed a version of an early mind-map may help in this.

The details contained in a chronology are a matter of personal choice. The document will change as information is gathered and clarified. Too much information will render the document less useful; details could be lost and linkages missed.

A chronology is a useful tool to use when speaking to witnesses as it can help them focus on key dates and to place events in order. _However, make sure that a witness or suspect does not see matters you would rather they did not see at that stage._ You might have to prepare a special revised edition for use at an interview with the suspect. Finally, a complete version of the chronology should be included as an appendix to your final report and referred to throughout the text.

POINTS TO PROVE

Another concept designed to focus the mind and assist the progress of the investigation is 'points to prove'. What are the points necessary to be proven to ensure that the case of misconduct is established against the employee? In Case study 1 they are the contractual terms or rules relating to hours worked, the fact that the employee (Simon) was late (either by personal observation or a witness), the company rules regarding signing in and that he was aware of them, and if applicable, evidence that he signed in falsely.

How would an investigator (although this might seem a grand title in such a relatively simple matter) set about proving these points? The times of duty will be set out in the employee's contract of employment, 'section 1 statement' or offer letter. These documents should be in the personal file. The fact that the employee arrived late would be established by direct witness evidence. The facts may be admitted by the employee but for this purpose we shall assume the matter has to be proven. The company rules on signing in and out should be obtained and attached to the discipline report. Finally, there is a need to prove that the employee knew of the rules regarding signing in. This could be satisfied by producing the signed checklist completed during the induction process.

This is a methodological approach taking each point at a time. However, the manner in which evidence is gathered is not always logical and predictable. For example and using the simple case study, what if we cannot readily trace the contractual details in the records? Is the discipline offence arriving late or signing in late? In actual fact it is both, but they are connected. Arriving late is the original discipline offence. Signing in at an incorrect time is the second offence, but only becomes such when you can prove that the time entered in the book is earlier than the actual time the employee arrived, and you would do this with a witness who saw him arrive at a particular time. This may seem petty but it is the basis of proving offences. Looking at ancillary issues like making entries in official records to cover misconduct such as lateness, financial irregularities or overtime can be proved by using Poirot's methodology of 'motive, means and opportunity'.

In Case study 6, theft of stationery, it is not sufficient to prove that the stationery items were found in the employee's rucksack; it must be established that they came from the stationery store, belonged to the company and the employee had no authority to take them. The more perceptive of my readers may be saying that in employment cases the standard of prove is only a 'reasonable belief'. It is a reasonable belief based on a reasonable investigation. Surely it is better to do the job properly when possible and avoid any room for argument or challenge if this is possible.

While dealing with 'points to prove', I cannot stress enough the need to obtain, secure, reinforce, or at the very least protect, your evidence. Relevant documents such as expenses forms and checklists should be seized. Documents that cannot be seized, such as entries in official ledgers, should be copied and signed by a witness. Files on electronic devices, including discs, memory sticks and so on, should be seized. Files on hard disks and servers should be isolated and secured; IT staff will help in this regard. There is nothing more frustrating that to return to collect evidence and find it 'missing'. There may be people other than the suspect who have something to gain from 'lost evidence'. This usually happens only once to an investigator; can I prevent the 'once' by this advice?

TRICKS AND DEVICES

Occasionally an investigator will find the going tough: evidence to support the facts or your suppositions is hard to come by, or witnesses, for whatever reason, are reluctant to get involved. Anonymous tips may not be transformed into usable evidence. Complainants may have 'thought twice' and reconsidered their allegations. If you find yourself in this position do not be tempted to resort to inducements or by spreading misinformation.

The power of the team can be quite strong and people can demonstrate a degree of loyalty in quite severe circumstances such as bullying. This, of course, includes resistance against any pressure from supervisors or managers who feel they could be seen in a critical light as a result of the investigation.

You can only do your best and report on what you find. Any attempts by the investigator to influence the investigation in an inappropriate manner can result in problems at any hearing or over employment tribunal claims, and put a dent in your reputation.

CUSTOM AND PRACTICE

When confronted with an allegation of malpractice, failure to follow agreed operating procedures or administrative requirements, employees can raise the defence of custom and practice. In practical terms this is to suggest that the activity or omission complained of is standard practice. For example:

- Employees were always allowed to take clothing graded as 'second quality' (as defence to an allegation of theft).
- The accounts office never asked for receipts (as defence to an allegation of excessive expense claims).
- Mechanics were always allowed to maintain their own vehicles in quiet periods.
- A grievance based on the fact that the senior accountant was always promoted to a manager vacancy.

The claim can also be made by management in response to a grievance raised by an employee, such as:

- Although there is no mobility clause in the contract, staff have always worked at other shops in the region to cover leave and sickness (a grievance about being moved temporarily to another shop).
- It is customary to take extra holidays between Christmas and New Year without taking normal allocation of leave (a grievance about days off being deducted from annual holiday allowance).

There is an old landmark case in this area (_Sagar_ v _Ridehalgh & Son Ltd_ [1931] Ch 310, Court of Appeal), based on weavers having deductions in their pay for bad work, which defined the basis for custom and practice. For a custom to have legal effect, in respect of discipline or a grievance, it must be 'reasonable, certain and notorious'. 'Reasonable' is a word used in all areas of law and it has never been defined with precision: simply put, it means what it says. 'Certain' is taken to mean that the practice happened all this time or it was very rare that it did not. 'Notorious' is taken to mean that it is well known by employees, managers and employers.

In legal terminology, the burden of proving a custom and practice is upon the party seeking to reply on it. In practical terms, however, a good investigator should look into the matter if this is raised as an issue.

FRAUD INVESTIGATIONS

This type of investigation is difficult and time-consuming. In serious matters my advice is to seek professional assistance from the police, auditors, external investigators and so on. However, low-level fraud can and probably should be tackled by internal managers.

Before any problems arrive (and although it is outside the scope of this book), I feel it would be useful to include a few simple fraud preventive measures. For example:

▌ Create, develop and regularly review financial instructions and processes.
▌ Carry out periodic 'spot checks' even without apparent reason or suspicion.
▌ Set up a confidential process for staff to report any concerns.
▌ Be aware of finance staff under pressure, working late, reluctant to take annual holidays.
▌ Be aware of relationships with suppliers and so on.
▌ Develop strict processes for dealing with cash.
▌ Ensure that someone backs up every task in your financial arrangements.
▌ Instigate appropriate separation of duties.
▌ Ensure that all computers in a finance area are 'password protected' and that the automatic shut-off is used after a short period to prevent unauthorized access.

When allegations are made or suspicions are raised, take rapid and decisive action. You can always pull back from an investigation. It is dangerous to wait and see how things go. Any investigator should be aware that fraudsters will make it their business to know the computer systems intimately, and audit trails may be difficult to find – hence the need for experts in most cases.

If allegations of fraud are made the suspects should, in most cases, be suspended immediately to prevent any opportunity of obstructing any investigation. Evidence lost at the early stages can never be regained.

Make it clear in policies and procedures that fraud against the employer is not a 'victimless crime'. It affects business performance and job security. The risk areas at the lower level are overtime, expenses, dealing with cash, purchasing and supplies, and where relevant, commissioning work after tenders.

CV FRAUD

Another growth area that may test an investigator's skills is that of CV fraud. The indications are that this is becoming more common. We have stressed the need for robust recruitment processes, and this is part of this process. I would recommend several preventive measures, including:

▌ Always use an application form and do not accept CVs. This will upset the recruitment agencies but no matter.
▌ Check both academic (many third-class degrees become a first over a period of time!) and professional qualifications (especially membership grades).
▌ Always take up references.
▌ Explore time gaps in backgrounds.
▌ Understand that occasionally the whole document and application will be bogus.
▌ Scan the application form or CV and ask pertinent questions in an interview.

If the applicant does get through the recruitment process there is still time to revisit the details, particularly if the recruit does not match up to the high standards suggested by their application details. If there is a suspicion raised the matter should be investigated thoroughly.

10

Interviewing

INTRODUCTION

Equipped with all we now know about evidence and investigation skills, we need to look at the methods we use to get information from people. In simple discipline cases this might be little more than the signing-in book or clock-in card for an allegation of habitual lateness, or a statement from a supervisor or manager. It might include the complainant or victim in cases such as abusive behaviour, harassment, minor theft or discrimination. The complainant is most likely to be an employee but it might be a customer, supplier or client. My experience is that many potential witnesses do not really want to get involved in a discipline enquiry, even when they are the complainant. Many people just want the treatment they being are subjected to, such as bullying or harassment, to stop.

Interviewing is critical in all but the most minor of discipline cases. Developing a high level of interpersonal skills, and in particular interviewing skills, is an essential requirement in management positions. Being asked to undertake an investigation in another part of your organization can be quite a challenge for an inexperienced manager, and systematic use of the skills outlined here will help. For example, the interviews of employees subject to the allegations in Case studies 2 and 3 would be quite challenging for the novice investigator. Perhaps most difficult of all is that you will need to speak to the suspect and get their response to the allegations by answers to specific questions or a written statement.

Effective interviewing is a complex skill, and you will only develop your competence with regular practice, constructive feedback and reflecting on your efforts. There is no real alternative to practice, and you are advised to take every opportunity to develop your interviewing skills in recruitment, appraisal, grievance or discipline situations.

Interviewing is a practical skill which benefits greatly from reflective practice. You will be aware that dealing with people, especially when they are under pressure, is demanding. I have to concede that some people have natural ability but everyone can improve with practice. Good interviewing is all about asking the right questions, listening and concentrating, focusing on your evidential objectives and being able to adapt your plan and questions in response to the answers you receive.

As managers you should seek out opportunities to conduct interviews and reflect on your efforts afterwards. Remember that learning from experience means developing and repeating tactics that went well throughout an interview. Equally, it is about reflecting on what did not go so well, understanding why and resolving to improve next time. Ask yourself, did I achieve my evidential objectives and did I arrive at the truth?

The main objectives of an interview conducted during a discipline investigation are:

- to gather information in order to progress an investigation by supporting, or alternatively disproving, an allegation;
- to provide information in order to plan or replan the focus and direction of an investigation.

RETRACTING A STATEMENT

From time to time a witness will ask to retract a statement or specific comments made in interview notes, or the person who is the subject of the investigation may retract a statement or answers given to questions posed during an interview. In these circumstances you should reinterview them, take another statement or a new set of interview notes. You should ask why they wish to retract their original statement. There could be a variety of reasons, which include threats or other inducements, and may lead to further lines of enquiry. Of course, they will be unlikely to admit this!

The investigator must retain the original statement or interview notes and include the second (or third) set in the file. The investigator must resist any pressure from a witness to destroy any original statement or interview notes. Further investigation or supporting evidence may indicate later which version is to be believed. Of course, they could all be fictitious! The final decision on which version to believe is taken by the disciplinary panel or, if the matters goes that far, the employment judge.

'NEGATIVE' STATEMENTS

Occasionally a witness will deny seeing or hearing anything relating to an allegation or matter under investigation. The investigator should take a brief statement to this effect and retain it on file. If the witness later 'remembers' certain facts, the original statement could be used to challenge their position. This could be seen as a cynical tactic but it often proves very useful and takes little time. A failure to see or hear what happened is not uncommon in bullying, harassment, health and safety contraventions, or failures to follow standard operating procedures.

Obviously an investigator should not put pressure on a witness but others might. A short statement denying any knowledge or even being at the scene of a particular incident takes very little time and could be priceless later.

ANONYMOUS WITNESSES

Best practice guidance about using anonymous witnesses has been developed in various cases. It is only acceptable to use statements in which the interviewee cannot be identified where a *genuine* fear of intimidation and retaliation exists.

Where the employer seeks to rely on evidence from an informant who wishes to remain anonymous, the accused employee is disadvantaged as they cannot challenge that evidence. In the landmark case *Linfood Cash & Carry* v *Thomson* [1989] ILR 235, guidelines were set out on the approach to be adopted, and it is worth quoting them in full:

1. The informant's evidence should be recorded in writing, usually in statement form and made available to the accused employee. It may be necessary to omit parts of the statement to prevent identification of the witness.
2. The statements should contain details of:
    i)   dates, times and places of any incidents;

ii) the opportunities and ability to observe clearly and with accuracy where relevant (eg whether the incident happened in the dark or at a distance);

iii) circumstantial evidence such as why the informant was alerted or can remember matters, for example knowledge of a system;

iv) whether the informant knows the accused or has suffered at the hands of the accused or has any reason to fabricate the evidence.

3. The employer should investigate the information to see whether it stands up and whether corroboration is available.

4. The employer should make tactful enquiries as to the character and background of the informant or witness.

5. Anonymity is acceptable where the informant does not wish to attend a disciplinary hearing and the employer is satisfied their fear is genuine.

6. If the employer decides to proceed with the disciplinary hearing then the chairman of the hearing should interview the informant and assess the credibility and weight to be attached to the evidence.

7. If matters arise that should be put to the informant, the disciplinary hearing should be adjourned for this to take place.

8. The witness statement, with omissions to avoid identification, should be made available to the accused.

9. If the employee or their representative raises any point which should be put to the witness, the hearing should be adjourned for this to be done.

10. Full and careful notes should be taken at the hearing.

Another case (*Ramsey* v *Walkers Snack Foods Ltd* [2004] IRLR 754) involved a group of criminals working together in a food processing plant to cheat customers out of valuable prize coupons in the packets. A full investigation was commenced and it soon became clear that those not involved were frightened to provide evidence. The company invited employees to call a telephone hotline with information. The HR manager was the sole contact with the employees and anonymous statements were used. Contrary to accepted procedures, copies of the anonymous statement were not supplied to the accused nor were the witnesses called to the hearing. The accused and their representatives were shown copies of the statements at the hearing. The HR manager obtained replies from the witnesses to questions asked by the accused. The allegations were found to be proven and culprits were eventually dismissed. This was tested in court and found to be reasonable in such exceptional cases. This case went further than the 'Linford' case above but was only allowed because of the genuine fear of intimidation and reprisals.

COMMUNICATION AND EFFECTIVE LISTENING

The actual process of interviewing consists of posing questions, clarifying responses where necessary and, critically, listening. All the tactics and techniques are based on these fundamental skills.

Communication in any context can be defined as 'the art of being understood'. It is about:

▌ creating a rapport, as far as is possible in the time available and the circumstances of the interview;
▌ use of simple and clear language;
▌ leaving suitable gaps and pausing to allow the interviewee to speak;
▌ listening carefully;
▌ clarifying what is not clear;
▌ treating the interviewee with respect.

Communication is more about reception that it is transmission. The interviewee must understand the questions you pose and you must ensure you understand the responses. Those who are highly skilled in areas such as lecturing, selling and giving presentations may need to address the need to be quiet and listen. I like to use the term *active listening* to describe the process. This is different from a conversation between friends and colleagues who are often not really listening – they are waiting for their turn to speak. This is not good enough in an interview scenario. It is *not* about patronizing an interviewee, being aggressive or adopting dubious practices. If your questions cannot be understood, the answers will be less than useful.

Effective listening is an active process – *active listening* – keeping eye contact and – what many forget – showing that you are listening. Do not repeat questions that have been answered correctly, it suggests that you are not paying attention. Simple non-verbal techniques like nodding can give the perception that you really are taking notice and listening. Non-committal sounds like 'Em', 'I see' can help to establish and maintain rapport.

The best way of convincing an interviewee that you are listening is summarizing and rephrasing, for example, 'So, what you are saying is…'. This really works: there is no better way to convince someone you are really listening than to repeat back what they have said. It also has the added bonus of checking that you understood them and allowing everyone to catch up and reflect. This is useful tactic in most forms of communication.

While considering inter-personal skills, it is worth mentioning *silence*. Interviewees must be given time to answer a question. Furthermore, pauses and silence can be used to prompt more detail. However, the overuse of silence can be intimidating. The careful use of silence is another of these dual-purpose tactics: it gives you time to reflect where you are in the interview and reassess your next step.

When you reach the end of the process and embark on the evaluation stage, consider who did most of the talking. If it was you, the interviewer, then it would seem that your technique needs to be improved. Fifty/fifty is not good enough: 70/30 in favour of the interviewee is much better, 80/20 is better still. However, remember you need to retain some degree of control with the garrulous.

If you have a colleague accompanying you in an interview, the areas you might ask them about later in the course of your reflection should include:

▌ clarity of questioning;
▌ listening skills demonstrated;
▌ displaying positive body language;
▌ who did most of the talking.

QUESTIONING TECHNIQUES

Before we deal with specific interview techniques, I would like to provide some guidance on basic questioning skills. The questioning techniques used during an interview depend very much on the circumstances and the interviewee. However, here are some guidelines that describe the various types of questions available in most situations. At a risk of stating the obvious, do not forget to allow time for the interviewee to answer.

It is quite likely that suspect or an employee against whom an allegation has been made will be unwilling to sign a written statement or the interview notes. They may even be advised to take this course of action by a colleague or trade union representative. Do not be fazed by this, nor should you show anger or disrespect if this is the case. Remember, the burden on proof is on the party bringing the allegation: at this stage, the investigator. Natural justice tells us that a suspect is not required to prove their innocence. However, having said that, many will seek to do this and you must be aware of being sidetracked.

Avoid the use of too many _leading questions_ such as 'I believe you were in the workshop when the fight started. Is this correct?' 'Did you speak to the customer?' This practice could result in you being accused of putting words into people's mouths. You should proceed in a more orderly way, such as 'Where were you at time/date?' followed by 'Did anything happen at this time?' 'Would you describe what you saw?' 'Did anyone enter the office?' 'What happened then?' The difference between leading questions and closed questions is that the former usually contains the answer you are seeking.

Interviewees are confused by *multiple questions* such as 'I understand you work in the office and were there on time/date'. Where were you standing, who else was in the room and what did you see?' If you get any reasonable answer it could well be to the last part only, or the part of your question the interviewee feels they want to answer.

Closed questions, those that can be answered by 'Yes' or 'No', are not recommended in most circumstances because the answers can lack detail. They can be useful, however, when they come at the end of a probing sequence or a 'funnel'. A probing sequence, in an investigation interview, is when an interviewer is seeking to establish a particular point and follows a series of open questions by a closed question. For example, after questions about the use of time sheets, knowledge of the relevant procedures, this stage of the interview could end with 'Did you enter a false time on the time sheet?' – answer, 'Yes.' A funnel technique is simply a general question followed by a specific question, for example, 'What happened in the workshop?' then, 'Who did this?' or 'What happened next?' The next stage of the funnel is ask why, how or who. Finally the funnel is closed by a closed question to ensure that you understood.

The use of *open questions* is extremely useful, particularly at the beginning of an interview. These are the types of question that can only be logically answered by a sentence. They usually start with 'who', 'what', 'where', 'when', 'why' or 'how'. It is impossible, in most situations, to answer 'Yes' or 'No' to an open question. In fact, you will be in good company in this technique, as Rudyard Kipling's poem says: 'I keep six honest serving-men (They taught me all I knew); Their names are What and Why and When and How and Where and Who.'

Another type of question is the *aggressive, disparaging or stress question*. This involves challenging and contradicting a witness, putting them under acute stress. Some people argue that these are necessary to enable an interviewer to observe reactions. While they may be useful at some stages of an investigative interview, there seems limited evidence that they produce useful material and they could be challenged later. Interviews are usually stressful experiences, and modern thought is that witnesses react more positively when put at ease rather than put under additional pressure. If you are working with a colleague, avoid the 'good cop–bad cop' tactic, it should be reserved for television crime dramas and could lead to your tactics being challenged or criticized later.

Finally, remember that some of your interviews may be with witnesses or suspects who have a natural language different from that of the interviewer. Unless you are 100 per cent certain that your interviewee has a complete grasp of your language, you must use an interpreter. Experience tells me to add the proviso that you must ensure the interpreter understands the context of the interview and translates the question and answer precisely. Some interpreters with limited skills paraphrase what was said or put questions or answers into their own words; this could cause an investigator untold problems.

INTERVIEW TECHNIQUES

An important element of an interview, particularly one with someone you do not know, is the introduction, sometimes called ice-breaking. Some of the systems described below include specific advice on commencing an interview, but there is general advice I can give at this stage. Do not dive straight into the key questions you need to ask. Allow the interviewee to 'warm up'. Explain the process, as far as they need to know, ask if they are comfortable and if they are happy to go ahead. Try to get your witness talking. Remember, the one thing most people are willing to talk about is themselves and their interests. 'What do you do in the office?', 'Tell me how you got to know Susan,' 'You have been in the workshop for six · years, how have relationships developed over this period?' and so on.

TRADITIONAL INTERVIEWING

For many years 'traditional' interviewing has been used in most investigations. This style is typified by the *unstructured interview*. When conducting investigative interviews, traditionalists often have no strategy, no plan, no pattern, and if direct questions or bullying do not work, there can be little else. In addition, the information gathered in this manner can be affected by perceptions and personal judgements – by problems such as:

▌ **Mirroring/similar-to-me effect:** The more closely a witness resembles the interviewer in personality, values, attitudes or background, the more they are likely to be believed. The interviewer assumes that 'my way' of doing things is the right or acceptable way. Conversely, a witness or suspect demonstrating different values or attitudes could be easier to disbelieve. This is a dangerous position to find yourself in as an investigator.

▌ **Contrast effect:** This is a comparison of witnesses with each other rather than measuring against the facts you know or suspect to be true. Each witness must be accepted on their merits. Maintain your focus and concentration on the task of evidence gathering and seeking the truth.

▌ **First impression effect:** For example, at a first meeting an interviewer might see an individual as sloppy, uninterested and obstructive, and consequently conduct the interview with a negative bias. The opposite also applies. There are many studies to suggest that the man in the smart suit is more believable that the man with the tattoos. This effect can result in a self-fulfilling prophecy. Getting the answer you expect is not the same as getting at the truth.

▌ **Stereotype effect:** The observation of one particular trait suggests the individual carries other traits not observed. Sex, ethnic origin, marital status, age, disability or other social categories may imply behaviour not actually observed. It is not right or even safe to say that ethnic groups stick together or that women will always back each other in sexual harassment cases. Learn to be open-minded.

▌ **Negative information bias effect:** Interviewers give more weight to perceived negative points than to those that are more positive. This can impact on objectivity and can seriously prejudice a discipline investigation.

▌ **Fundamental attribution error effect:** Interviewers incorrectly assume that some action on the part of the interviewee is or was caused by an aspect of their personality rather than by a simple response to events: for example, nerves or bravado. An example could be that a young man with a reputation for having many girlfriends is thought guilty of sexual harassment. This could lead an investigator to fail to adduce the evidence necessary to establish guilt.

However, the traditional interview survives; some reasons are that interviewers are unaware of the higher success rates possible in other formats, or that some managers regard themselves as good intuitive interviewers who avoid the classic errors. The advice imparted in this book seeks to challenge this and offer an alterative approach!

Remember, if you only have a hammer in your toolbox then all you can do is to knock in nails.

WASP

Many practitioners follow an interviewing structure with the pneumonic WASP. This stands for:

- **Welcome:** An explanation of the purpose of the interview and the process of putting a witness at ease. Getting the witness to talk freely is not always easy.
- **Acquire information:** A questioning sequence followed by a witness statement if offered and appropriate.
- **Supply information:** The stage at which you give information to the witness, perhaps to allay their fears, put their mind at rest or assure them that action is being taken.
- **Parting:** a convenient word for telling the witness or suspect what happens next.

THE PEACE PROCESS

A third and more complex structure is the PEACE model, based on work carried out within the British police service. The process is equally useful with witnesses, complainants / victims or those suspected of a disciplinary offence. The mnemonic represents:

P plan and prepare
E engage and explain
A account
C closure
E evaluate.

Before dealing with each stage in turn, I declare my hand and commend this structure to you, particularly if you are charged with conducting anything other than a simple investigation. The extra stages are the keys to success both in the interviews you are conducting and in the development of your skills in this important area. I have used this many times over the years and found it to be practical, effective and logical.

Plan and prepare

Before getting down to the actual interview, it is essential to plan and prepare. Preparation is both a mental and an organizational task. You should always be well organized. If the pressure of time prevents this, you should at the very least always strive to give the impression of being well organized. This last point may seem out of place but I am aware that sometimes investigators are put under extreme pressure to carry out their work quickly, especially if an employee is suspended. There is a simple maxim that applies in many situations but particularly so with regard to interviewing:

Fail to prepare and prepare to fail!

The interview is usually a one-off opportunity to gather facts, test out perceptions already collected from elsewhere and obtain explanations. You may have to reinterview in investigation scenarios; however, this should be more the exception than the rule and should be avoided where possible. You should start off with the intention of only seeing a particular witness once, although you may have to review this principle from time to time. Witnesses, and in particular the suspect, may suggest excuses, defences or alibis that require further investigation. Remember what we agreed at the very beginning: your role is not primarily to build a case against the suspect – it is to seek out the truth.

If you are to conduct a disciplinary or investigatory interview with a potential witness, make sure you know the precise purpose of the interview and what your evidential objectives are. Make sure you have gathered and read relevant documents such as complaint letters or statements, work schedules, timesheets, relevant e-mails, standard operating procedures, guidelines, rules and regulations. If you are investigating a breach of rules, find out how and when an employee was made aware of the rule in question. It may have been included in the induction process, there may be a signed checklist, or it may be in a formal clause of the main terms of employment or contract of employment.

A competent interviewer should ensure that they have any documents that may be required to put before the interviewee for comment. You may do this by asking, 'Do you recognize this document?', 'Do you recall sending this e-mail?' or 'Is this your signature?' This is much better than referring to a document you do not have with you at the time of the interview.

In an investigative situation ensure that you are familiar with the organizational policies and procedures and any relevant codes of practice on dealing with discipline and grievance procedures. Failure to follow procedures could at the very least allow the main issues to be blurred by arguments on technical matters. At the worst procedural mistakes could result in decisions being overturned later in the process, and would certainly be challenged by trade union representatives.

This stage builds on the planning or mind-mapping explained in Chapter 9 on investigation skills and techniques. The chronology is critical in assisting you and the witness to place incidents in the context of a timeframe.

It is good practice to prepare a list of questions to put to a particular witness. If these are printed on a sheet do not forget to leave space for the answers. In addition, leave space for questions that may be necessary following on from what a witness might say. Their evidence or involvement may be more extensive than you originally thought.

I return to this topic in the final stage of PEACE but it is worth stating here and now that your plan, mind-map, list of questions and chronology are not carved in stone. Do not be restricted in your thinking by the plans you have made. A particular witness can, and often does, tell you something that has the potential to change your plans and refocus the direction you take in the investigation. Be prepared for this and do not close your mind to new lines of enquiry or evidence. At the same time, do not allow red herrings or false trails to detract you from your objectives. Remember what we said about some witnesses having their own agenda.

Engage and explain

The right introduction is crucial in any interview. First impressions are all-important. Introduce yourself, particularly if you are unknown to the interviewee, and also anyone else present. The interviewee should be made aware of the reason for the interview, your terms of reference (if applicable) and the procedure which will be adopted. We have discussed the ways you can 'break the ice' as a preliminary to a difficult interview.

It is critically important that an employee suspected of a discipline offence should be informed of the allegation(s) they face. This should have been done by the senior manager who appointed you as investigator. In some situations you may need to serve the documents yourself. Check before you start any interview. In most procedures it is normal for the suspect to be given details of the allegations before the investigation commences.

Always conduct the interview in a formal and professional manner. Bear in mind that your actions and demeanour may be reviewed elsewhere: for example, a discipline hearing, an employment tribunal or some other court of law. With the exception of very minor issues, it is not the role of the investigator to judge or pass sentence.

Account

This is the heart of any interview, and the stage at which the interviewer seeks to adduce facts to support or disprove the case. You should give some thought to the physical positioning of the interviewee, any other people present and yourself. Ensure that you are all comfortable and that potential interruptions have been removed, including mobile telephones. Avoid placing an interviewee facing a window where they can be seen from outside or distracted by what is happening outside. If it can be avoided, do not embarrass suspended suspects by asking them attend at their own workplace.

While a side-by-side position is better for counselling or appraisals, face-to-face is the more conventional mode for investigatory interviews. If you are to conduct a long investigatory interview, plan to build in comfort breaks, and if possible light refreshments – definitely no alcohol! If the interview is likely to take a long time, remember that some witnesses may need to take a smoking break.

You must always allow the interviewee to explain matters. Do not omit to explore, delve into, and if necessary challenge, information; especially inconsistent information.

The interviewer has a choice of approaches to take. If the interviewee is willing and able to respond freely, it is best to use what is described as a *cognitive interview* technique. This is where the interviewee gives their account with minimal interference. It is supported by the interviewer prompting recollection in different sequences or from different perspectives to check accuracy and stimulate detail. You need to develop the detail of the story and check inaccuracies. Do not rush the process. It may be useful to obtain a verbal description of events before starting to write a statement or your interview notes. If your preparation included some questions that were not addressed by the interviewee, these can be posed at an appropriate stage in the proceedings. Sometimes this process simply involves setting the interview in place and listening to the story.

However, interviewees are not always amenable to a cognitive interview; they may be reluctant, forgetful, confused or obstructive. In these cases it may be appropriate to use a technique called *conversation management*. This is a more directed approach for the reluctant witness. The interviewer should use a prepared list of questions and add probing questions at appropriate stages. In these circumstances a signed statement is unlikely and the interviewer, or their note takers, will need to record both questions and answers. Some interviews can be a combination of both techniques.

This type of interview could, in extreme cases, be a series of silences or 'No comment' replies. There is nothing you can do about this. You should continue to pose all the questions you need to ask, recording the response to each. Do not give up just because you keep writing 'no comment'. It will be the duty of any discipline hearing to make judgements on a suspect's answers. You cannot always rely on the suspect providing the evidence you need to prove the case.

Just because the suspect is not making any response (it is unlikely a witness would take this approach), there is no reason to terminate the interview. This could however be necessary if the suspect becomes violent or extremely obstructive, although this happens very rarely.

Finally, be aware that on occasions, emotions could run high. People could be in fear of their jobs and the personal disruption this may cause to them and their families.

Closure

At the end of the interview it is necessary to have some formal closure in addition to the signing of a statement, if one is obtained, or the written questions and answers.

Before terminating a witness interview, the interviewer should summarize and check what has been said. The witness may wish to know what happens next as far as they are concerned. In a discipline situation they may be worried how the material they have provided will be used. They should be told if there is a chance they may be called before a disciplinary hearing.

A suspect interview should also be terminated formally. They should be told that they will be provided with a copy of any statement and that the investigator will be reporting to senior management in due course. It may be useful and considerate to give some idea of the timescale if this is possible.

The interviewer/investigator should avoid any personal opinions or comments, particularly on what decisions they think may result from their report.

Evaluate

The evaluation stage is crucial and should never be missed:

1. There should be careful consideration of the information obtained, what is confirmed or corroborated or, conversely, what is thrown into doubt or contradicted. What facts can now be considered to be 'certain'?
2. Where do you go from here? What facts remain to be clarified or corroborated? What further action do you need to take? How does this impact on other interviews? These matters may require you to amend or redraw your mind-map or plan.

3.   From a personal development point of view, how did you perform? Did you deal with the task effectively, did you grasp every opportunity, or do you need to revise your tactics in future interviews? Develop the skills of a real reflective practitioner and use them every time.

WITNESSES

Witnesses are crucial in providing the reasonable level of proof to enable a discipline panel to make a finding of guilt. Bear in mind, however, that some witnesses will have an agenda, and be keen to give personal opinions rather than evidence to establish or disprove facts. Your questioning techniques should enable you to get to the truth, as far as is possible. The interview should seek to obtain full details of what occurred, what was actually seen or heard, the sequence of events, names of other people present and/or involved in the incident, facts the witness believes to be true, and as far as is possible, actual words used by key people. Witnesses should be reminded before making a statement that, in most circumstances, their evidence could be made available to the employee under investigation.

In some minor discipline cases the report of the manager or supervisor will suffice for the decision to be made. For example, in lateness or failure to follow procedures, the only statement necessary would be that of the supervisor or manager. In more serious cases statements would be required from victims (in cases such as discrimination, assault, harassment and bullying) and experts (in cases involving IT, technical issues or financial irregularities). Independent witnesses are always useful in giving a 'fly on the wall' view of what happened. In criminal investigations independent witnesses are particularly welcome. However, in employment discipline cases or investigations into grievances, it is difficult to find a witness who is truly independent. Employees work together and know each other well, many will have had previous altercations, and an investigator needs to be aware of the problems bias can create in the truthfulness of the statement.

To highlight this remember the story about the football supporters and the genuinely different recollections of an experience. Try to get witnesses to describe what they gathered directly from their senses, what they saw, heard and so on. An investigator should be careful when asking witnesses to interpret what they saw or heard or to give reasons for what someone might or might not have done.

How many witnesses do you need? This really depends on the complexity of the issue, whether the facts are in dispute, whether the allegation relates to a series of incidents. If you are unsure obtain more statements than necessary while memories are fresh. A decision to discard them can be made later.

Vulnerable witnesses

Generally speaking a witness has no right to be accompanied. However, it may be good practice in some circumstances. If you are a male investigator, it would be unwise to interview a female witness in a sexual harassment case without a female colleague in attendance. Similar circumstances could appertain in cases related to race, ethnicity or religion. Dealing with employees whose first language is not English will present its own challenges. In addition, it is good advice to interview a young witness, or an employee with a learning disability, in the company of an appropriate adult.

SUSPECTS – THE DISCIPLINE INTERVIEW

Before dealing with the interview, we ought to revisit the possibility of an employee _remaining silent_ throughout the interview or giving 'No reply' answers. This may happen when discipline proceedings are running concurrently with a police investigation and an employee has been advised (probably correctly) to remain silent so as not to prejudice their position. There is a criminal precedent in that when a defendant fails to give evidence, answer questions or raise a defence until late in the process, they may be subject to a court drawing an inference of guilt. A similar inference would not, I suggest, be unreasonable in the employment cases.

In an employment context, an employee's refusal to take part in the employer's investigation does not mean that a dismissal, even before the outcome of a criminal trial, would necessarily be unfair. Furthermore, an acquittal in a criminal court would not make a dismissal, based on the same or similar facts, unfair, as the standard of proof is less stringent.

In practical terms, if there is a parallel criminal investigation, it may be necessarily to discuss the progress of an internal investigation with police so as not to inhibit or prejudice their work. However, there is no obligation to do so, and as we have agreed, there is no requirement to report a crime to the police. It is quite common for employers to decide to deal with matters such as minor theft or false expenses claims internally. I have been surprised when some employers have chosen to deal with serious matters internally. Some feel that involvement of the police or other official bodies would impact negatively on their image or customer relations. An investigator can only do their best and not be surprised if any recommendations are not followed.

Should the investigator operate alone? Obviously this depends on the resources available and the nature of the investigation. Most evidence gathering can be done alone. However, it is good advice to appoint someone to take notes during interviews, particularly in more serious cases. It is essential that an investigator is accompanied at an interview at which the interviewee is accompanied. An investigator should never allow a 'two to one' situation as this can lead to unnecessary and distracting challenges later.

Having a note taker enables the interviewer to concentrate on establishing rapport, observing body language, putting interviewees at ease and thinking of additional questions. In addition, it can assist the investigator to keep a track on the point or points they are attempting to prove and to vary their questions based on the responses given.

The timing of an investigatory interview with a discipline suspect is critical. The investigation should be held before memories fade, or in some cases evidence is lost accidentally or intentionally. It makes sense to have carried out all the preparatory work mentioned above. You would normally have interviewed most, if not all, of the witnesses. You should be in a position to plan carefully your approach and many of your questions.

Arrange the mutually convenient time, date and location of the interview. The location of the interview should be carefully selected, away from the normal place of work if possible, and where interruptions can be eliminated. Bear in mind that the suspect may be subject to suspension from work, in which case an interview away from their workplace, and unless they agree to be interviewed there, away from their home, will be necessary.

Remember you may need to arrange for your note taker and for the suspect's workplace colleague or trade union official to attend (if required).

It may be that the suspect has reported sick. In this case you should be careful not to be seen to apply unnecessary stress. The employee must agree to the interview, and particularly if the sickness absence is due to a mental or psychological condition, the advice of their doctor should be sought. Again, the investigator should balance a considerate approach with the need to prevent delaying tactics.

It is a clear requirement of best practice that employees are given every opportunity to state their case. It is also important that the employee is clear that this is an investigation, that at this stage no decisions will be made, and the employee is not at immediate risk of dismissal or other disciplinary action.

An investigator is duty bound to follow up any reasonable line of enquiry the employee may raise in their defence or in mitigation.

NOTE TAKING AND STATEMENT WRITING

After interviewing a witness you should complete interview notes or draft a statement unless it is clear that they have no relevant evidence to contribute to the enquiry.

However, having said this, I would like to add a cautionary word and show my cynical nature as an experienced investigator. Some witnesses can change their mind over details and also suddenly remember what they were previously unable to recall. _If you have any reason to suspect that this may be the case you should write a negative statement._

INTERVIEW CHECKLIST

- Prepare, prepare and prepare.
- Control the environment.
- Structure the interview.
- Vary your questions.
- Listen to the answers and probe for detail.
- Keep it relevant.
- Remember it is a two-way process.
- Leave on the right note – tell the interviewee what is to happen next.

STATEMENT OR NOTES CHECKLIST

In more usual circumstances the statement should be written on a form similar to the witness statement form in Chapter 14 or one dictated by company procedure. A witness statement has the following basic content:

- Name, address (if not an employee), their position in the company, where they work, and briefly what their duties entail.
- Where the witness was at a particular time and date, or over a period of time.

▌ What the witness saw or heard of relevance to the enquiry (based on their answers to your questions). If in doubt about the relevance, adopt an inclusive style as opposed to exclusive: that is, if in doubt include the detail.

▌ All the events and actions written in chronological order.

▌ A reference to any documents shown to the witness, such as 'I have seen the timesheet showed to me by the investigator, Mr Smith. It is the one I authorized with my signature on [date]'. In some complex investigations it may be useful to use exhibit numbers for each document.

▌ The actual words spoken by the witness should be used if at all possible, and should be in quotation marks.

▌ Opinions should be avoided unless the witness is qualified to make them. For example, a quality inspector may state that a piece of work is sub-standard, a health and safety officer make state that a certain procedure is unsafe.

End the statement by having the witness sign at the bottom of each page and at the end of the document. They should sign an endorsement such as, 'This statement is true. I make it of my own free will and I have been told I can alter anything I wish.'

If you record interview notes – many investigators do this – it is a good idea to use the document on which you have set out your prepared questions. Leave space for the answers and for additional questions that may occur as the interview progresses.

Whether you obtain a written statement or record answers to a series of questions (interview notes), you should get the document signed by all those present.

If you do use notes and have left spaces that are unused, it is good practice to draw a line through the spaces when the document is signed to avoid any suggestions that additional material was added after the interview had concluded.

You may be under time pressure, but do not be tempted to telephone or e-mail a potential witness to send you a statement unless you have no alternative. In addition, do not be persuaded to write a statement yourself and send it to a witness for signature without an interview. Either of these situations could bring your professionalism and impartiality into question.

ADMISSIONS AND CONFESSIONS

These concepts originate in criminal law. However, I feel that it is worth explaining the basics and how they fit into your investigation.

An *admission* is when the person under investigation admits certain facts. This could be verbally in response to questions, and entered on interview notes or in a written statement. It is common for there to be several admissions. For example:

'Yes, I was at work on 27th February.'
'I spent all day in the office; I even had my lunch at my desk.'
'I did speak to Mary in the photocopying room.'
'I did enter the cost of the meal on my expenses claim.'

However, these admissions of certain facts you may be seeking to prove are often followed by a denial of other facts. For example:

'Yes, I was at work on 27 February. But I did not speak to any one from Brown and White Ltd.'
'I spent all day in the office; I even had lunch at my desk. I never spoke to Peter.'
'I did speak to Mary in the photocopying room. The conservation was about general matters and I did not make any indecent remarks.'
'I did enter the cost of the meal on my expenses claim but only after the sales manager had instructed me to do so.'

An admission can save you the trouble of proving certain of your 'points to prove'. Taking the photocopying room admission above, which could involve an allegation of indecent behaviour: you do not need to prove that the man who made the admission was in the photocopier room at the same time as Mary – it is admitted. You still, nevertheless, need to find evidence of the alleged behaviour.

A *confession* is much more; it is a full acceptance of all the facts support-ing the case. For example: 'Yes, it was me wot done it guv, you have me bang to rights.' For our purposes, I treat a confession as an admission of guilt or an acceptance of responsibility. Confessions are made frequently, sometimes followed by mitigation or excuses. You need to be extremely careful in dealing with a statement by a suspect, as it may not be all it appears to be. For example, a statement such as, 'Yes, I did kiss Mary in the photocopier room. But it was with her full consent and participation' is admission of certain facts but not a confession to the allegation of inde-cent behaviour, or indeed indecent assault.

Another problem with admissions and confessions, particularly the latter, is that they can be challenged later. For example:
'I did not say that.' Or 'I did not mean that.'
'I only admitted the allegation because you told me no action would be taken against me.'

Even in a discipline hearing, a careful defence can result in the admission or confession being excluded from the evidence. If this does occur and you have no other evidence your case could be lost.

RECORDING INTERVIEWS

The rules regarding the recording of interviews with suspects in criminal investigations are well established, and many agencies use videotaping. A similar level of formality is not normally necessary in a discipline situation, but it might be if the matter under investigation is of a criminal nature. If it is decided an interview should be taped, you would be well advised to use a proprietary tape machine made for this purpose. These machines are designed to record two separate tapes simultaneously, one of which could be provided to the employee. It is not unknown for some trade union rules to ask for tape recording of interviews in more serious cases – perhaps where dismissal could be an outcome.

Investigators should remember that the transcribing of tapes is a time-consuming and expensive process, and should be avoided in most cases.

As an investigator you may wish to use a small cassette-type recorder to assist in note taking when interviewing witnesses. If you do so, you are advised to make this clear beforehand. These tapes should not be used as evidence unless the witness agrees. They are used more as an *aide memoire* in drafting a statement for signing later. This is not advised when interviewing suspects, when the normal question and answer followed by a written statement would be safer.

While on the subject of recording interviews we ought to mention covert recording. This activity moves the investigator into a complex situation and may involve breaches of human rights. I would leave this to law enforcement agencies, where the use of this technique is only allowed with the highest prior authority.

NEGOTIATION

Generally speaking negotiation is not part of the investigator's role. However, there are occasions on which some degree of negotiation may be useful to achieve the greater purpose. For example, an employee may be on the very periphery of a general unworked overtime scam, theft of company property or false recording of hours worked. It may be necessary to offer a promise not to take disciplinary action for a minor breach, or agree a lesser penalty in order to gain evidence against a ringleader. Sometimes young employees are dragged into discriminatory practices against their wishes, for example, against a fellow employee because of the employee's sexual orientation. Use of their evidence against the major offender could be the only way justice can be done, and the employer is able to enforce its duty of care against the employee being discriminated against, particularly when it is reduced to one person's word against another's.

Do not use these tactics unless you are confident in your role and have the prior agreement of the senior manager sponsoring the investigation. You should never hold out promises to witnesses that you are ultimately unable to uphold.

11

Report writing

INTRODUCTION

The final stage of the investigatory process is the report. It is the aim of this section to give you the skills to do justice to your investigation in the submission of a cogent report. At the end of your investigation it will be necessary to report to the disciplinary officer who will chair any discipline hearing. Depending on the nature and extent of the case under investigation, the report could be a few pages or a comprehensive document with sets of statements and exhibits. It is important that you take care to ensure the report is carefully prepared and contains all the necessary detail. The essence of a report or a letter is to communicate at a distance. This requires careful thought, and planning your writing to take account of the needs of your readers. I would also remind managers about to submit discipline or grievance reports that the document will have a great deal to say about the competence and professionalism of the author.

Ask yourself, are there areas that need to be explored or revisited in light of subsequent information? Do you have enough background? Have you sorted out your documents, interview notes and statements? On the other hand, if you feel you have done the job, submit the report promptly.

There may be a format in your discipline policy or an accepted way of setting out management reports in your organization. Do you know a reliable colleague who has submitted a discipline report which you could use as a template? There is no sense in reinventing the wheel.

Personally, I would never think of starting a report or complex letter without constructing a mind-map, or maybe a series of mind-maps. I find this to be a very useful tool through which to gather my thoughts, set out a sequence and put the various items in place.

I have mentioned this technique before, and Figure 11.1 shows a simple mind-map. Most of mine are a little more complex. However, it does give an example of the method. The one you work from in planning your might be the final drawing of several attempts to get things in order. It is a personal choice, but I find it extremely useful.

DISCIPLINE REPORTS

A great deal of what I have to say in this section in terms of concepts and techniques applies to all writing. A discipline report is submitted to enable a senior manager to make a decision in the following range:

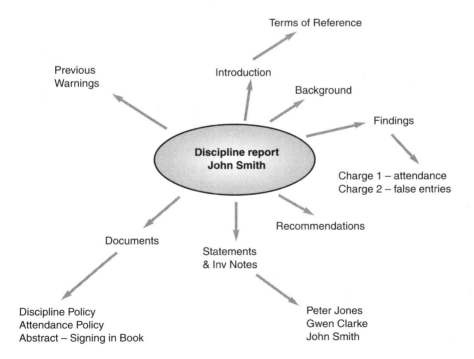

Figure 11.1 A simple mind-map

■ to find sufficient evidence in the report to hold a discipline hearing in respect of all or some of the allegations that are the subject of the investigation;
■ to arrange for the person who is the subject of the investigation to be given a warning about their future conduct;
■ to take no further action.

Some disciplinary officers are keenly aware of the political implications of a discipline investigation, particularly involving senior people, and take a wider view of the specific issues involved in the report. To this end the disciplinary officer may require that you (the writer) submit a draft report, and might subsequently ask for certain parts of it to be changed. This is a situation that you can only deal with at the time. This challenge has faced the author as both an internal manager and an externally appointed investigator. It is virtually impossible to give specific advice in these circumstances. Bear in mind that you will have to present the report to the discipline panel and you may be required, in exceptional circumstances, to justify your report at an appeal or in a court of law.

CONCEPTS

The basic concept is to seek and set out the truth. It is to be fair and logical. If there is genuine doubt about a particular fact and you cannot reasonably resolve this doubt, the person under investigation should be given the benefit of the doubt. If you cannot establish a fact so as to create a reasonable belief that it is true, your report should say so. It is important to be balanced. If there are matters in favour of the person under investigation they should be included even if not entirely relevant. If the information given by a particular witness is critical but you have some doubt about their truthfulness you should say so, even if it weakens your case.

The concept of 'plain English' is important in all business writing, and I include a few specific suggestions in the next section. I have already made the point that communication is the art of being understood. If a reader has to read a particular paragraph twice in order to be clear about the meaning, or they have to consult a dictionary, I would suggest you have failed with this type of document. The acid test is whether your report could be understood at first reading in the way that you intended it should.

A final concept is to be concise. You do not have the time to produce an unnecessarily long report and the discipline officer will not have the time to read it. Do not repeat yourself by saying the same things in the introduction, findings and summary. Obviously your report needs to be complete but good planning should enable you to deliver this to a reasonable length.

TECHNIQUES

First, you must ensure that the *grammar and spelling* are correct. Do not rely on a computer spelling and grammar checker, they will let you down. I know that it is notoriously difficult to proofread your own work but in these circumstances confidentiality may mean that you have to do so.

In order to improve the *readability* of your report you should use short sentences written in plain English rather than long sentences in complicated language.

You must avoid *ambiguities* in your writing. This requirement applies to your report and also to the way you interview witnesses, write interview notes and statements. For example:

I have heard others make comments about the girl in accounts.

Who actually said what, about whom and when?

The petty cash tin was kept on the desk, on top of the filing cabinet or on the window ledge.

Where was it at the time in question?

The atmosphere in the office was fairly good, there were some disputes but not many. Some people didn't see eye-to-eye.

What does this mean?

I try to manage the use of the photocopier. I know it is against the rules to make any personal use. I allowed the secretary to copy some dress patterns and I have copied a couple of articles from a holiday magazine. I even let Mary copy one of her son's university essays but when Peter copied the whole of his car's handbook I thought I should take disciplinary action.

This last quote was contained in a supervisor's disciplinary report I received some years ago.

Finally, *simplicity* is the key. Use short sentences with simple words, where possible without loss of precision. Avoid padding out your work by phrases such as:

- 'on a regular basis' (use 'regularly');
- 'due to the fact that' (use 'because');
- 'in the vicinity of' (use 'near').

FORMAT

The actual layout, in terms of headings and so on, may be constrained by the rules set out in a policy or by the normal way reports are submitted in your organization. Some large organizations have computer-based templates containing fonts, formats, headings, numbering and so on. Some will require a specific hierarchy of numbering using a combination of numbers and letters. If not, I recommend a simple approach. I would use a font such as Times New Roman or Arial and a size of 11 or 12 point. A line spacing of 1.5 or double makes a long report easier to read but it should not be used in a letter. Paragraphs should be headed in bold and numbered. The use of a numerical system, such as 2.3, 2.2.3 etc, makes it easier to insert paragraphs and move them about the report. The numbering of each paragraph is optional. Personally, I find it a little tedious unless it is a complex document.

The basic layout of a discipline report should be something like:

▌ Introduction
  – background, but not too much detail: the senior manager will know most of the background;
  – terms of reference
  – complainant – where relevant, it might be discipline instigated by a management colleague;
  – employee(s) – the subject(s) of the investigation;
  – allegations or charges;
  – acknowledgements.
▌ Summary of evidence
  – agreed facts or admissions;
  – a brief outline of the evidence.
▌ Findings and conclusions
▌ Recommendations
▌ Appendices
  – chronology;
  – documents and exhibits;
  – interview notes and statements.

This is not a definitive format and you will develop your own style. For those of you new to this type of work, this could be one less problem to resolve.

STARTING THE REPORT

The first part of your report will be the *introduction*. Before you start, you should be aware that your report could be scrutinized by an employment tribunal or other court. In these circumstances it could be disclosed to lawyers representing the employee or ex-employee.

The rationale of any discipline or grievance investigation is that it should be thorough, fair, reasonable and consistent. It is worth repeating that you are not trying to build a case against anyone but to ascertain the truth and support it by the best evidence you can assemble. If you have followed the guidance in this book you should have carried out a professional investigation and be in a position to reach some form of conclusion.

The introduction should be brief but contain the *background* of the incident or situation under investigation. This should contain enough detail to enable the reader to develop a picture of the situation and circumstances in which the allegations took place. For example, in allegations of racial harassment in an office or workshop there should be a description of the racial mix, the atmosphere and any relevant issues or allegations.

The introduction should contain details of any *complainant* and the relationship with the suspect if relevant. Allegations such as poor attendance or theft may not have a specific complainant. There should be details of the *person under investigation*.

The *allegations or charges* should be listed, and in the case of multiple suspects, should show which charge is alleged against which employee.

The *terms of reference* should be set out and mention should be made of any limitations they contain.

Sometimes the introduction contains any *acknowledgements* that the investigator may wish to express. This might include support from human resources/personnel, a translator, the IT technician and so on.

The next section is usually a *summary of evidence*. The idea is to briefly outline the evidence contained in the report and, maybe, any limitations in the evidence. This section could contain a list of *agreed facts or admissions* made during the process. This is a legal tactic that can save time and space. The agreed facts and admissions should have been signed by the employee under investigation, and as such there will be no need to provide evidence of them. You will recall reading about admissions and confessions. Examples could include:

▌ John Smith was on duty in the workshop all day on Wednesday 24 June.
▌ John Smith was working on project 21/08 with Imran Khan all day on Wednesday 24 June.

▌ John Smith had been appointed by the Company to mentor Imran Khan throughout his probationary period.

▌ John Smith admits that he was given a verbal warning for failure to follow standard operating procedures, in failing to secure the lathe safety frame, on 12 March.

These admissions and confessions could be many and varied, but if they are agreed there is no need to include evidence in your report to prove them. You may wish to include any *mitigating factors* in your summary. I prefer to leave them until the end, and I shall return to these later.

The next section is usually the *findings and conclusions*. This is a systematic examination of the investigation and the evidence gained. This section will contain many references to documents, interview notes and statements contained in the appendices. It will involve the reader referring to these supporting documents frequently. It should highlight any corroboration and supporting evidence, by other witnesses or by documentary evidence. It should also highlight any inconsistencies and ambiguities that could not be resolved.

You have the option to either deal with each allegation in turn, each employee in turn (if there is more than one suspect), or tackle the incident in one block. In complex case I prefer to deal with the situation as it develops, then address each allegation in turn.

In dealing with each allegation you should arrive at a *conclusion* based on the evidence you have obtained and explained in your findings. You will recall our discussion of the standard of proof necessary in employment cases in Chapter 9. This concept may be relevant in your drawing a conclusion.

Before I proceed to deal with *conclusions* I ought to mention that some organizations require an investigation report to omit this stage and leave the drawing of conclusions to the discipline officer. This is more the exception that the rule, and in any event the discipline officer is not required to accept the conclusions drawn by the investigator.

In a disciplinary report, and often in a response to a grievance, the following terms are used to signify a conclusion:

▌ A finding of *unfounded* is made if there was no evidence that the alleged offence took place. This really means that there is no evidence to support the allegation. In addition and in some cases, it may prompt further work to ascertain whether the original allegation was malicious.

▌ A finding of *unsubstantiated* is made if the alleged offence may have taken place, but there is not enough evidence to conclude that the alleged offender committed the alleged offence. You may recall that, in order to prove a case, there should be evidence that the matter took place as alleged: for example money was missing from the petty cash box during the period in question. In addition, there must be evidence that the suspect committed the offence. Both elements need to be established such as to be reasonably believed. If you achieve one element without the other the matter is unsubstantiated. In effect, the investigator is saying that there is insufficient evidence to instigate disciplinary action.

▌ A finding of *substantiated* is made where there is evidence, usually with corroborating testimony from witnesses, that an offence as alleged was committed by the alleged offender. Bearing in mind the standard of proof necessary, this is saying that, in the opinion of the investigator, there is enough to proceed to a disciplinary hearing on this matter. This, of course, is not the investigator's decision to make.

The report might end with a statement that the conclusions applied to this report are based on a review and assessment of:

▌ the allegations;
▌ the evidence and any inconsistencies in the evidence;
▌ the facts, provided and admitted.

It is sometimes the case that the findings produce evidence of other cases of misconduct not included in the original list of allegations: for example, that a case of sexual harassment was in fact an allegation of indecent assault, that the investigation resulted in other 'suspects' being revealed or that the charges ought to be framed in a different way. These, and the evidence supporting them, should be included in an interim report to the discipline officer. The discipline officer may wish to extend the investigation, amend the charges or commence a parallel investigation. The investigator should not make amendments to charges without authority. Natural justice requires that an employee must know the nature of the allegations made against them and have an opportunity to put forward an explanation.

Recommendations are fundamentally different from conclusions. It is likely that an investigator will be expected to draw conclusions from their findings. However, it is less likely they will be asked to make recommendations. If in doubt about this point you should check. A recommendation may be an opinion whether a disciplinary hearing action should be held or not, or what penalty might be imposed.

MITIGATING CIRCUMSTANCES

While some people would leave mitigation to the employee under investigation and their representative, it is part of the investigation and should be included in the investigator's report to fulfil the duty to be fair and balanced. It is part of the investigator's duty to ascertain the facts rather than construct a 'prosecution case' against the employee. Mitigation is not, technically speaking, a defence to a discipline charge. It is defined by *Collins English Dictionary* as 'circumstances that may be considered to lessen the cupability of an offender'.

In practical terms, mitigation can be related to the incident or disciplinary offence itself: for the want of a better term, this is *situational mitigation*. There are many examples of this, such as:

- 'I did throw the wrench at John but he had been on at me all day about my football team losing in the Cup' (hardly sufficient to warrant any lessening of penalty).
- 'Yes, I was operating the machine without the guard. However, I was always taught to do it this way as it takes less time' (possibly suggesting a warning and a training solution).
- 'I did refuse to go to the sales conference with Peter but, and I have not said anything before, he has been asking me for a date for the past six months' (if true reasonable and a case to look at against Peter).

Personal mitigation relates to the employee. This can range from the fact that they have an unblemished record to suggestions that the employee is suffering from work-related stress. Examples are:

- 'I have been late several times over the past few weeks but my partner has been in hospital and I have had to take our children to school' (could and probably should be a welfare solution).

As we have seen the standard of proof is one of reasonableness, and this also applies to the weight to be given to mitigating circumstances. The mitigating factors may not be mentioned during the investigation and only arise at the hearing. However, if a mitigating factor brought up at the hearing is more like a defence, the question may be posed why it was not mentioned at the time of being interviewed about the incident.

The *appendices* to your report should include the *chronology* we have discussed. Obviously this will be of more assistance in the more complex cases and in simple cases it may not be necessary. Nevertheless I would strongly recommend getting into the habit of producing a chronology in every case. A further section should include all the *documents and exhibits* relevant to the case. These could be policies, procedures, e-mails and letters. They should all be given a reference, and the number reference should be included in your report, interview notes and statements at the point at which that particular document or exhibit is referred to.

Finally, the appendix should contain all the *interview notes and statements* relative to the case. You may have undertaken more interviews than are included in the file. If these are of no evidential value they could be omitted. There may, on occasions, be more concrete exhibits such as weapons, defective pieces of work and damaged laptops. It is common-place to use a photograph in the exhibits folder. The actual article could be produced at the hearing if necessary.

EXTRANEOUS ISSUES

There may be a need to include matters not associated with the actual discipline case but associated with it and arising out of the investigation. These could include recommendations for changes of policy or standard operating procedures, the introduction of new forms or records, training matters or even suggestions of physical changes in the workshop or office. You may need to take advice on how these are to be reported. I would suggest a separate report to the appropriate senor manager or employer. A suggestion that a procedure needs to be amended could be seized upon by an employee as to some degree reducing their level of guilt.

PLEA-BARGAINING

Although this sounds like a concept more at home in a criminal than an internal discipline enquiry, it can have a place. Occasionally a particular allegation against an employee cannot be proven to a satisfactory level – that they can reasonably be thought to be guilty. The facts may not be available to the investigator, witnesses may be reluctant or selective in their memory or the employee may be particularly good at covering their tracks. It may be thought better to have a warning on the record of a diffi-cult employee rather than fail to establish a more serious offence. For example, where a contravention of standard operating procedures results in injury to another, it may be easy to accept an admission to failing to follow procedures when evidence of reckless behaviour is not available. There are many examples of suspected fraud ending up as a failure to complete required records.

The decision to go along this track is not one for the investigator although they would have a contribution to make. The disciplinary officer should be involved, and where appropriate, the employee or their repre-sentative.

12

The discipline hearing

INTRODUCTION

Once you have submitted your report the next stage is out of your hands, although you may be required to present the case if a hearing is held. This chapter looks at the whole subject of discipline hearings including receipt of the report, the decisions that need to be made, the processes to follow and the hearing itself. It will be of assistance to managers who may be required to sit on discipline panels in addition to covering the duties of the investigator at the hearing.

THE DISCIPLINARY OFFICER

The disciplinary officer is the term used to signify the person appointed to hear the discipline case and chair the discipline hearing. The advice from ACAS and also under natural justice is that the disciplinary officer should not be the line manager of the employee under investigation or the investigating officer. It is recognized that in some smaller organizations it might need to be the same person. The disciplinary officer's duties are to receive the report, review the evidence contained in it and make a decision as to the next step. The normal options, in respect of each allegation and each 'suspect' are:

- Return the report to the investigator to clarify certain points or conduct any further investigation that seems to be necessary.
- Take no further action. Decide that the report does not contain a prima facie case against the employee, or any particular one if there are more than one, and that the matter should be dropped.
- Decide that there is no case worthy of a discipline hearing and the matter should be resolved by issuing a warning as to future conduct.
- Decide that a disciplinary hearing should be held on some or all of the allegations.

Any hearing must be conducted in good faith. The panel should resist the temptation to take action for reasons other than those forming the allegations or to produce a predetermined outcome. It would be wrong to take disciplinary action when the evidence does not justify it to demonstrate, as in Voltaire's quip in _Candide_, that in England they find it necessary, from time to time, to execute an admiral 'pour encourager les autres.'

THE PANEL

A disciplinary officer can sit alone but it is better to form a panel of at least two. The company policy may indicate the number and grade of discipline panel members. In addition the policy may indicate that only certain grades have the authority to dismiss. If the case involves some form of discrimination or harassment, or issues of a technical nature, such as health and safety breaches, it may be wise to include a specialist in this field. In many organizations a senior member of HR supports the panel as an advisor.

ADMINISTRATION

Before the hearing, the employee under investigation (and their representative) should be supplied with all the documents relating to the allegations. This includes all statements and interview notes, all relevant documents and exhibits and any agreed list of admissions or agreed facts. This does not include the report submitted by the investigating officer, although matters such as mitigating circumstances and personal details could be supplied. You may recall we discussed anonymous witness statements but these are very much the exception.

The chairperson should be familiar with the discipline procedures and ask HR to obtain the personal file of the employee. This should contain any previous warnings which are still live. Generally, it is not lawful to act on previous warnings that have expired: for example, a written warning left on file for 12 months should not be mentioned after this period.

The disciplinary officer should decide which witnesses to call to the hearing. Some organizations use only written statements or interview notes. There may be some discussion with the suspect and their representative as to which witness interviews can be read out and which should be heard in person. The final decision rests with the chairperson. However, natural justice requires that the employee should have the opportunity to challenge any allegations made against them.

Arrangements should be made in respect of venue, time and date to ensure that all parties are available. It is normal practice to accept one request for a change of date and time by the employee and then hear the case in their absence. However, common sense should prevail, and it should be considered how it would look if an employment tribunal reviewed the decision some six months afterwards!

The venue should be secure, private, quiet and without interruptions. This may present problems for a small employer. There is no problem in hiring a room in a hotel or similar. It is normal to have someone taking notes of the proceedings.

THE HEARING

The hearing is under the control of the chair, usually advised by the HR representative, and should take the following course:

1. Immediately prior to the hearing the chair should ensure that all the papers and documents are in place and there are sufficient copies. No documents should be produced that have not been previously supplied to the employee and their representative because this will undoubtedly cause a delay in the proceedings.
2. There is usually an opening statement by the chair, introducing all present, especially anyone who is not known to all such as an external specialist or a regional trade union official. This statement usually reinforces the purpose and nature of the hearing and that the outcome could be disciplinary action.

3. The chair should take care to ensure that an employee who does not have a trained companion (a trade union official) knows that they can ask questions and make observations.

4. The investigating officer then presents the case against the employee. This involves introducing the evidence generally and then either reading statements and interview notes or calling witnesses to give evidence verbally. Relevant documents or exhibits should be introduced at the point they are referred to by a witness. Incidentally, witnesses should only be called into the hearing to give their evidence, and after any cross-examination should be released and asked to leave.

5. The cross-examination of witnesses by either side is a matter for the chair. It is common to allow this as long as the process is not oppressive. However, there is no legal right to cross-examine a witness in this type of hearing.

6. The employee should then state their case and call any witnesses. Of course, if the witnesses are employees, the employer should have made all necessary arrangements to enable them to attend. If cross-examination is allowed, the investigating officer may ask questions. If the employee under investigation refuses to address the panel or to answer questions, the matter should be decided on the facts available at the time.

7. The chair, or any member of the panel, can ask questions.

8. The chair should be aware that it may be necessary to adjourn from time to time for a variety of reasons such as:
   - the employee seeking a private consultation;
   - to deal with any complaints made by the defence as to the arrangements or the procedures;
   - to take legal or procedural advice from the HR representative;
   - calls of nature or refreshments.

9. It is normal to hear any 'situational mitigation' at this stage.

10. At the end of the evidence the panel will normally adjourn to consider its verdict.

11. The panel then reconvenes and announces its verdict on each of the allegations and against each of the employees under investigation. The panel hears any personal mitigating factors, any previous relevant warnings, and adjourns for the final time to consider its decision.

12. On reconvening the panel announces its decision. The penalty should be in accordance with the policy and should show some degree of consistency within the organization. The options are verbal warning, first and then final written warning, and dismissal. If the circumstances warrant it, there is no problem in moving straight to a final

warning without having to progress through all the options. Decisions such as suspension without pay or the imposition of a fine are only legal if they are contained as options in the employment contract.

13. Under normal circumstances the decision and penalty are announced on the same day. There is no legal requirement to do this but it seems only fair to inform the employee of their fate. If the chair of the panel is not authorized under the organization's policy to dismiss and this is the decision of the panel, there would need to be an adjournment to seek a ratification of the decision by a senior manager having the authority to dismiss.

14. Finally, the panel should inform the employee of a right to appeal and then confirm the decision in writing.

PRESENTING THE CASE

This book is primarily about managers undertaking disciplinary action or investigating discipline allegations. It seems appropriate to give some advice about presenting the case to a hearing. Some managers may find this duty onerous.

First, if an employee is represented by a workplace colleague or trade union official, it may be useful to agree any preliminary points and non-contentious issues beforehand. This may be set out in an agreed admissions and facts document to be presented to the hearing.

The key to success in this arena is preparation. You must know the policy and procedure, be familiar with your report and evidence, and if possible, the room in which you are to present the case.

A technique used by lawyers in presenting cases is *signposting*, in which they give an indication of where they are going, what topics they are to cover and in what order. This makes following the case much easier. It is usually better to present the case in a chronological order. You should ask the panel to refer to your chronology. Make sure the defence have a copy, which should have been agreed before the hearing. Do not overdo the introduction. Identify the areas in which there are disputes and indicate where decisions are required. Finally, don't waffle or spend minutes sorting through bundles of paper.

When presenting a witness, let them give their evidence themselves, unless they are nervous and need guidance. In cross-examination listen to what witnesses are saying, take note of any contradictions and ambiguities, and ask short, clear questions. Always be aware of the points you are trying to prove and their relationship to what is being said.

Finally, be courteous and fair to everyone, especially the employee subject to the allegations. Remember, your task is to seek the truth.

THE ROLE OF THE REPRESENTATIVE

Any workplace colleague or trade union official representing an employee in discipline hearing has a specific role to play. Trained trade union officials know what they should be doing, and when they are not trying to push the boundaries a little, they assist in maintaining fairness and adherence to procedures. They will also have had the opportunity to study the statements, interview notes and documentary evidence. Some representatives may have conducted a parallel investigation.

Representatives are allowed to ask questions and make representations. If the chair allows a cross-examination, the representative can do this. Employers, in the guise of discipline panel chairs, are not obliged to allow those who have complained about an employee's behaviour to be cross-examined by that employee. However, they may be obliged to do so where a proper investigation requires complainants to make their statements before employees (*Dolan* v *Premier International Food Ltd* [2005] All ER (d) 152). The representatives are not allowed to answer questions on behalf of the accused employee.

The investigator should be aware that the trained representative will be looking for the very gaps I have been mentioning throughout these chapters, such as vague or ambiguous evidence, options as opposed to facts, hearsay evidence (which as you may recall is things said and done not in the hearing of the accused employee) and contradictory evidence from any source. The representative will be seeking to discredit a witness by trying to get them admit to personal animosity or prejudice towards the accused employee.

In addition to attacking witnesses who are called to give evidence in support of the employer's case, the representatives will be seeking to highlight situational factors that could be seen to have an effect on the allegations. These could include staff levels, colleagues off work sick, lack of training, poor supervision and inadequate or unclear policies. It would be useful for the investigator to be aware of the nature of these challenges in order that they can obtain facts to support the organization. This may not always be possible!

The chair will need to control the debate in any discipline hearing and prevent the case from descending into a slanging match. I have been involved in such hearings and it does little to benefit the employee under investigation.

We have mentioned the fact that the process may need to be adjourned to deal with procedural matters. However, the employee may seek to submit a formal grievance against anyone involved in the process or the procedure itself. In most cases it will be necessary to adjourn or suspend the hearing pending resolution of the grievance. If a grievance is not addressed at the time and subsequently found in the employee's favour, it could cast doubt on the hearing itself and any decision made as a result of it. Of course, this could be a delaying tactic, and this is discussed in the next section.

DECISION MAKING

The panel will need to make a decision on each allegation based on the evidence presented before it at the hearing. We have covered the standard of proof required in discipline cases. It may be useful to expand a little on the term 'reasonable' at the stage of the final decision, particularly if the panel is considering a dismissal. The test of reasonableness is, in the circumstances (including the size and administrative resources of the employer's undertaking), is there sufficient reason to dismiss the employee? The question should be determined in accordance with the equity and the substantial merits of the case. This means the fairness of the decision and the reasonable belief in the facts supporting this. Is the panel sure that the investigation has been thorough and fair? It has been held that a small employer is not absolved from the need to carry out basic procedures such as an investigation.

The legal position on the decision made by a discipline hearing is quite clear. Was the decision to dismiss within the 'band of reasonable responses' open to a reasonable employer? If the case does reach the stage where it is argued at an employment tribunal, the tribunal cannot substitute the decision they would have made (*Post Office* v *Foley, HSBC Bank* v *Madden* [2000] IRLR 827, CA).

A recent case (*Dr Ryta Kuzel* v *Roche Products Ltd* [2008] EWCA Cic. 380) argued in depth about the decision to dismiss an employee. A summarizing quote by the appeal judge is useful, 'An employer who dismisses an employee has a reason for doing so. He knows what it is. He must prove what it was.' This should give clear guidance to a panel in reaching its decision.

Finally, there is a need for an employer to maintain consistency across the organization in the way it deals with and adjudicates on disciplinary matters.

PROBLEMS IN THE HEARING

When dealing with suspension in Chapter 5, you may recall I mentioned that employees may resign while under investigation. This sometimes occurs during a discipline hearing, often following an adjournment and discussion with a representative. If this happens after consultation with a trade union official, it should be accepted. You may wish to conclude the hearing and reach a verdict in principle.

If the offer to resign is made by an unrepresented employee, my advice is to adjourn the hearing and give them time to reconsider their position, and perhaps seek advice. Some discipline panels do offer an employee the option of resigning but this should be done with care, possibly after legal advice. It is not advisable to give an employee grounds for a constructive dismissal claim.

If an employee is ill for a short period the discipline hearing should be rearranged. However, if the illness is for a prolonged period this may raise additional problems. The employer is entitled to ask the employee whether they are fit enough to attend the hearing. Medical advice may assist in this matter. If the employee is on a period of long-term sickness and it is not thought appropriate that they should attend the discipline hearing because of physical or psychological issues, the hearing should not be held. The employer should take into account any prognosis on recovery, and if appropriate, consider dismissal for medical incapability.

Obstruction by the employee, such as refusing to attend the hearing or disruptive behaviour during the hearing, should be dealt with by the chair on its merits. If after warnings and a rescheduling of the hearing, the problem continues, the employer would be entitled to hear the matter in the employee's absence.

There is a great deal of law surrounding discipline hearings (including dismissal), and if the panel follows this guidance, it should, as far as is possible, avoid any of the pitfalls.

A discipline hearing is a serious business and it should always be borne in mind that the employee could lose their livelihood as a result. Employment law, best practice and official guidance are constantly changing and all those involved need to be aware of the current situation.

The competence of the investigator, the professionalism of the disciplinary chair and the thoroughness of the supporting policies should ensure that there is balance and fairness at all the stages. A decision should be based on the facts and a reasonable response to the facts. Remember, it is important to be reasonably certain that the incident took place *and* that the accused employee was responsible for it.

After a disciplinary hearing has been held there should be review and a process of reflective practice. Talk through the experience, ask questions and review actions. Are there any lessons to be learnt? Do any policies or procedures need to be reviewed? Remember, there is as much to be learnt from what went right as what went wrong, and many organizations only seem to learn from the latter.

DISCIPLINE APPEALS

It is an established and fundamental principle of good employment practice and of natural justice that employees should have the opportunity to appeal to the employer against any disciplinary decision, or a decision based on a formal grievance.

Ideally an appeal should be heard by an independent senior manager: that is, one who was not involved in the line management, investigation, discipline hearing or grievance decision and has had no prior involvement in the case in question. Obviously this is not possible in a small organization, and the law acknowledges this. Some form of independent arbitration may be suitable, or someone from outside the organization could be asked to chair an appeal if both sides agree.

Grounds for an appeal

The normal grounds for an appeal are one or more of the following:

▌ The process was flawed, there were procedural irregularities, it was unfair or contrary to company policy. Did the failure to follow a procedure have a material impact on the case and the decision?
▌ The investigation failed to discover the true facts or was biased, prejudicial or not carried out in good faith.
▌ The original hearing was not held in good faith: for example, the outcome was predetermined.
▌ Additional evidence has emerged since the hearing. This does not make the original decision unlawful but it may give the employer an opportunity to right a wrong if this is the case.
▌ The decision made at the original hearing was not a reasonable and fair conclusion from the facts before the hearing.
▌ The decision did not take sufficient account of matters such as a confession, an apology, previous record or other mitigating factors.
▌ The decision was inconsistent with other decisions under similar circumstances anywhere in the organization.

Holding an appeal hearing

The same administrative processes regarding notification and right to be accompanied apply as they do in respect of the original hearing. An appeal is not normally a second run of the whole process, although in exceptional circumstances it could be.

The rules of natural justice apply to appeals as they do throughout the disciplinary process. The appeal should be heard without undue delay, there should be a right of representation by a workplace colleague or a trade union official, the right to be heard in good faith and an opportunity for the grounds of appeal to be heard by the employer.

Many organizations treat an appeal as a paper exercise by hearing the representation of the appellant and then considering the statements, interview notes and any notes made of the original hearing. Bear in mind that many organizations do not call witnesses to discipline hearings.

In employment, civil and criminal courts, subject to certain conditions, any side can appeal. At the risk of stating the obvious, it is, in my experience, unknown for a manager to appeal against a decision to find a discipline case not proven.

The first stage is for the appellant (the employee or ex-employee) to give the grounds on which they are submitting an appeal. There should be a reason or reasons they are dissatisfied or disagree with the decision made, usually one of the grounds listed above. In respect of an appeal against a decision based on a formal grievance, it is usually because the employee does not accept the decision made on the original grievance. I find that some appeals throw in everything but the kitchen sink. The appeal challenges the investigation, the investigator, the procedure, the findings and the decision. It is unusual to call witnesses to an appeal unless there is new evidence to hear.

The second stage is for the panel to consider its decision. It may ask the investigator to respond to the matters raised by the employee, but again this is uncommon. It is highly unusual for the appeal panel to ask the manager who heard the original hearing to address it.

Decision of an appeal

There are a range of decisions an appeal panel can reach after hearing an appeal.

It can *reject* the appeal in its entirety and confirm the decision made by the original discipline hearing. This decision should also be given in writing and with reasons. In most situations the decision of a disciplinary appeal is final. If the decision goes against the employee, or ex-employee (they may have been dismissed), they have no option other than to seek advice on the possibility of submitting a claim to an employment tribunal; this is outside the scope of this book. It is unusual for more than one appeal to be allowed against disciplinary action in any organization.

If an appeal panel rejects an appeal against a lower-level decision on a grievance there may be other levels. This depends on the grievance policy, and some large organizations have three or four tiers before a decision becomes final.

It is open to a disciplinary appeal panel to *overturn the decision* of the hearing and find the case against the employee not proven. This may involve reinstatement if they are suspended or re-engagement if they have been dismissed. I must add that this does not happen very often! Of course the panel may make different decisions on different charges if the case is more involved.

More frequently, an appeal panel *replaces a decision* by the disciplinary hearing by substituting a lesser penalty. This could be replacing a dismissal by a final warning or a final warning by a first warning and so on. In theory, and unless the policy prevents it, appeal panels could replace the original decision by a higher penalty, such as a final warning by a dismissal. I have never known this to happen in my considerable experience.

I have known an appeal panel decide to order a *new investigation* when it is dissatisfied with the original one after hearing the submission of the appellant.

Finally, an appeal panel might, and often does, add a rider about review of policies or procedures.

FOLLOW-UP

It was a challenge where to place this short section; I decided to include it at the end. I could go on at length on these matters but I feel that a brief mention will suffice in this context.

Discipline is not a common occurrence in most organizations, whether they are small or large. This is especially the case if the process involves a dismissal. It is almost unknown for the facts to be kept secret. and even worse, if the real details are unknown, other than maybe the fact that a dismissal has taken place, the grapevine will work to create a good story. There may be a need to issue a short statement to set the facts straight, particularly if a complainant is still in post.

The first issue is *learning from the experience* both at the organizational and the personal level. I have stressed reflective practice throughout the book and I feel it is a critical development tool.

At the *organizational level*, the need to take disciplinary action is, in many circumstances, symptomatic of a system failure. This could be in job analysis, recruitment, failure to follow effective induction or probation processes, poor management, a lack of proactive discipline and so on. Managers need to reflect on this and make an attempt to identify the weaknesses in their systems. Of course, this reflection may involve some people accepting blame or criticism, and this is sometimes necessary before an organization can move on.

Managers should be careful in moving employees around after a discipline case. This could be seen as victimization if a complainant is moved to a different job or area without their consent.

At the *individual level* this may involve a new experience or reinforcement of established skills. How was it for you? What did you learn from the experience, what would you change the next time you are required to investigate a disciplinary case, and why? How are your investigatory, interviewing and report writing skills?

At the *team level* there may be issues that need to be addressed. Are the team happy with the result or was the dismissed employee popular? Some rogues are well liked! Is the man or woman who made the allegation of harassment genuinely unpopular? Do you need to undertake some serious team building? Is there a need to reinforce standards? Is it time you changed to a philosophy of *proactive discipline*?

Finally, is there a need to *review policies and procedures or training provision*? It may be worth meeting with other managers and human resources, if you have this luxury, to discuss any changes.

Dealing with discipline is not easy. Balancing the grievance of an employee against the needs of others and the organization is often difficult. I hope I have given sound advice and guidance in addition to giving some useful tactics, checklists and procedures.

13

Case studies

It might be helpful to illuminate the issues raised in the chapters by the consideration of some realistic scenarios. All are fictitious but reflect issues and problems that I have seen over the years.

Case study 1   Simple discipline (lateness)
Case study 2   Internal grievance (sexual harassment)
Case study 3   Grievance and discipline (bullying)
Case study 4   Discipline (false expenses claims)
Case study 5   External complaint of sex discrimination
Case study 6   Theft

The problem with case studies is that they can never tell the complete story unless they are too long to be useful. There will always be elements of the situations you will not be aware of, questions you would want to ask and personalities you would like to know more about. However, the basic procedures are set out for your guidance, and to place many of techniques and tactics explained earlier into the context of an actual discipline or grievance:

▌ Remember you can always retreat from a discipline approach. It is more difficult to move to a discipline investigation from the starting point of treating a situation in a casual way.

▌ You should not rant and rave at an employee, or give them 'stern words of advice' and then proceed to discipline. You must choose one or the other, although I have found the aggressive rebuke less than effective in the long term.

▌ Take a systematic approach and follow your own procedures.

▌ Keep records and reinforce _proactive discipline_.

CASE STUDY 1 – SIMPLE DISCIPLINE

The facts

You are the manager in an insurance brokerage, a subsidiary of a large company. You have been the manager for two years and have a staff of five. Two are in a job-share arrangement and the others full-time, working contracted hours 8.30 am to 5.00 pm with an hour for lunch. They cover six days a week. Those working Saturday are granted a day off in the week in addition to Sunday when the office is closed. As the manager you always try to be friendly, fair and well liked. You have never taken formal disciplinary action against anyone before.

Simon is one of your full-time insurance clerks. He deals with all matters but specializes in motor insurance. He has been with the company for five years and is a competent worker.

When your staff arrive and leave they are required to sign an attendance book. Simon has always had a casual attitude to work and from time to time you have had to mention to him that he has been a few minutes late. You also had to mention that Simon signs himself in at 8.30 am even when a few minutes late. This sometimes causes customers to wait when several call into the office on their way to work locally.

At your last annual appraisal meeting with the regional manager you were criticized for allowing discipline in the unit to drop a little. The manager quoted examples such as dress standards especially on Saturday, staff timekeeping and staff telephone manner sometimes being too casual. You accept this criticism and agree to work at this area of your duties.

You are aware that Simon has recently moved in with his girlfriend. One particular week you observed that Simon's actual arrival times were Monday 8.42 am, Tuesday 8.59 am, Wednesday 8.30 am, Thursday 8.45 am and Friday 9.15 am. In view of your appraisal you decide that the matter is unacceptable and needs to be dealt with urgently and formally.

You check the signing book to discover that Simon is signed in at 8.30 am on every day this particular week. You ask Simon to meet you in your office. You point out the facts as you see them and ask for an explanation. He tells you that he often has trouble parking his car, and in any event, the others do not work as hard as he does. He does not apologize but says that he will try to be on time in the future. In accordance with the company policy you warn him about his future conduct. Your company policy states that informal warning can be given by the immediate line manager but formal warnings and other action, including dismissal, can only be dealt with by the regional manager.

Two weeks later Simon is 8 minutes late on Monday and 15 minutes late on Wednesday. What do you do?

Options

1. Ignore the matter. It might not happen again.
2. Give Simon another informal warning.
3. Tell Simon off in front of his colleagues with the intention of embarrassing him into compliance.
4. Investigate and report for a discipline hearing with the regional manager.

I hope you would take Option 4. Options 1 and 2 could show the manager as weak and indecisive, particularly in view of the warning at his appraisal. Option 3 could work but think of the impact on Simon, the rest of the team and your credibility as a manager. Remember, you should praise in public and criticize in private.

Checklist

▌ Check the signing-in book and photocopy the relevant entries (whether false or not!).

▌ Arrange a meeting with Simon, although it is not required by law. Check your policy to see whether he should be given the option of being accompanied. Obtain a copy of his contract of employment, offer letter, 'section 1 statement' or company rules relating to times of work. In addition, obtain a copy of the induction checklist signed by Simon after the rules regarding signing in and out had been explained; this should be in his personal file.

▌ Point out the facts of the alleged misconduct, supported by the documentary evidence, and ask for an explanation. Depending on the facts, there could be two charges: first, simple lateness (which is misconduct) and second, possibly falsification of records (which could be gross misconduct).

▌ Note his reply and inform him that you are to report to the regional manager.

▌ Submit report with supporting documentary evidence.

Although this is a relatively simple matter and to use the word 'investigation' is a little grand, it is good practice to follow the correct procedure. It will demonstrate competence to your line manager and establish a good methodology if or when you are required to tackle more complex matters. You have gathered a mixture of direct and documentary evidence.

Points to prove

The _points to prove_ are the contractual terms or rules relating to hours worked, the fact that he was late (either by personal observation or a witness), the company rules regarding signing in and that he was aware of them, and if applicable, evidence that he signed in falsely.

You should be aware that if a colleague signed in for Simon this could also be treated as gross misconduct and extend your investigation. It might be misguided loyalty but also shows a disregard for company rules.

Your report should be relatively straightforward. In most cases it would be inappropriate to include a recommendation although some senior managers would require this. If you are unsure, ask! Finally, you should adopt a balanced approach and include any comments you have regarding Simon's performance generally.

Remember, you may be required to present this report verbally to any subsequent discipline hearing. Although you may think this is a relatively minor issue, falsification of company records and repeated misconduct could justify dismissal.

Finally in this set of circumstances, you may have to deal with a different relationship with your staff after this change in your enforcement of the rules.

Before leaving this first case study, you may recall that earlier in the book I suggested an alternative outcome to this, where Simon finally admitted he had to take his partner's child to day care. This is a good example of how you can retreat from discipline to welfare but not in the other direction.

CASE STUDY 2 – INTERNAL GRIEVANCE

The facts

This is quite different from internal discipline. You are the owner/manager of a small company supplying building materials. Your cash sales assistant asks to speak to you in private to make a formal grievance. She is obviously upset. In brief, she complains of sexual harassment over the past two months by John Hopkins, a local builder and regular customer. She tells you that Hopkins has been asking her for a date, despite the fact that they are both married. He has sent her suggestive notes, and recently has taken to sending indecent e-mails. In addition, he makes comments about her dress and figure in front of other members of staff and customers. She brings with her some diary sheets and copy e-mails. The e-mails do contain indecent and totally inappropriate comments. How do you deal with this matter?

Options

1. Tell her not to be so sensitive and that 'men will be men'. Maybe she should take it as a compliment.
2. Point out the fact that Hopkins is a good customer who pays his bills on time; for the sake of the business and her job she should accept his banter and not get upset.
3. Remove the problem by finding an excuse to dismiss her.
4. Investigate the grievance and deal with it in a positive manner.

I hoped you would take Option 4. I do not know which is the least dangerous of Options 1–3 but I know of instances when each of these has been seriously considered and in one case used. Remember that failure to deal with this type of grievance could lead to constructive unfair dismissal and litigation, which would be almost impossible to defend and potentially very expensive. The pressure on a business not to alienate a good customer should never be enough to ignore a serious grievance from a member of staff. Remember you have an implied contractual duty to provide a safe working environment.

Checklist

▌ Ask your employee what she wants you to do about her grievance; she may just want it to stop. There is the possibility it may be false, exaggerated or a misunderstanding but you _must_ treat it seriously and deal with it promptly, sensitively and in private. You may want to refer back to my comments on difficult conversations in Chapter 2.

- Make sure she does not have to deal with Hopkins while you investigate. There may be a case for a temporary transfer to a 'behind the scenes' position or even special leave, on full pay. Make sure that she is not treated badly following her grievance – this could amount to victimization and further grounds for a claim.

- Make notes of the allegations. A full statement may not be necessary at this stage but, if you progress to a full investigation, you will need a full statement before memories fade.

- Investigate the matter, speak to witnesses, and obtain and secure the notes or e-mails relevant to the allegation. Depending on the size of the company you may want to appoint a manager to investigate. However, this is a serious allegation and should not be given to an inexperienced manager.

- You will need to speak to your customer Mr Hopkins. Your employee may agree to a face-to-face meeting with him to discuss the matter, but in most cases, this will not be acceptable to either party. It should not, of course, be imposed on her. Of course, you risk a total rejection by Hopkins and a removal of his business.

- If there is a case to answer, you must take action to protect your staff. This may be to refuse to deal with Hopkins or at the very least remove your employee from the source of the complaint. Do not take the side of Hopkins unless there is clear evidence of a false allegation. In this unlikely event you may need to consider discipline against the clerk.

- Make notes of your actions and retain on file. Make sure that you, or a manager, monitor the situation to ensure no further cause for complaint. Inform your employee of what you have done and ask if she is satisfied.

There are no points to prove in this scenario. Harassment is defined as 'any form of _unwanted_ verbal, non-verbal or physical conduct of a sexual nature.' Failure to deal with this problem could be a serious matter. The only real defence that Hopkins could put forward, in light of the e-mail evidence, is that your employee encouraged this attention and, for some reason, later decided she was 'in too deep.'

Incidentally, if there is a suggestion that this behaviour continued outside the workplace, you might consider reporting it to the police.

It is unlawful for an employer to fail to take reasonably practical steps to protect employees from harassment by third parties where such harassment is known to have occurred on at least two other occasions. There are two particular situations to consider here. First, the employer must react positively to complaints from employees and take clear action. As in other areas of law the term 'reasonably practicable' is not defined and is a matter of the circumstances. The second obligation on employers and managers is to be aware of situations that could give rise to complaints of this nature.

In April 2008, the Sex Discrimination Act was further amended to change the definition of sexual harassment and to include for the first time employer liability for third-party harassment. This legislation is relatively new and there are no binding appeal decisions to give guidance. However, as we have seen, the intention of the person making the statement is irrelevant. From the perspective of our subject area, complaints in this area must be investigated and dealt with.

CASE STUDY 3 – GRIEVANCE AND DISCIPLINE

The facts

You are the technical director of an engineering company and have been so since you formed the company with three colleagues 20 years ago. You are responsible for the computer-aided design office and the workshop. The other directors are the managing director, sales director and finance director. The workshop is managed by Paul Green, a very experienced and competent engineer who was promoted to workshop manager some 18 months ago after starting with the company shortly after its inception. There are two overseers, Peter Black and Charlie White, one dealing with large one-off projects and one with small production items.

The workshop is busy and often works under time pressure to get projects completed on the tight schedules set by the sales team.

You are aware that the culture of the workshop, which is totally male-dominated, is aggressive, loud and at times confrontational. You know that Paul Green is finding his management duties difficult and can often be found operating one of the lathes or a precision finishing machine.

You receive the note below addressed to you and headed 'Personal and confidential'.

Mr Waters, Technical Director

As you know I have been working in your workshop for some nine months. I have always tried to do my job correctly and I try to assist others when I can. Generally speaking I have been happy at your firm. However, matters have become so bad that I feel I must write this note.

The supervisor in the workshop, Peter Black, is making my life a misery. He is aggressive towards everyone, especially me, and his attitude is getting me down. I have taken some time off sick recently but I cannot afford to lose pay. I think he dislikes me because I am younger than the others and I do not take part in their banter.

What do you do?

Options

1. Tell him to 'grow up' and stand up for himself.
2. Tell him that you are happy with the supervisor; you know he is a little rough but he gets the job done.
3. Transfer the worker to another job.
4. Investigate the allegation and deal with it in a positive manner.

Again, I hope you would take Option 4. Remember that failure to deal with this type of grievance could lead to constructive unfair dismissal and litigation. You might recognize that the employee making the grievance has less than one year's service and is not entitled to make a claim to an employment tribunal of unfair dismissal. You could reject his grievance and then decide he is unsuitable and dismiss him with notice. Is this the culture you really want to engender in the organization?

Checklist

▌ Is this a case when management might consider suspending the supervisor? It may not be appropriate but it should be considered: refer to Chapter 5 for guidance on this. Depending on the severity, it may be necessary to isolate one employee from the other, at least during the investigation period.

▌ Is this a case that your policy requires to be allocated to a manager from another area?

▌ As before, ask the complainant what he wants to be done. He might just want the bullying to stop. There is the possibility the complaint is false, exaggerated or a misunderstanding but you _must_ treat it seriously. Bear in mind the possibility of victimization. If it transpires that the bullying is based on the fact, or even the incorrect assumption, of the complainant's sexual orientation, ethnicity or even his age, the matter takes on a more serious perspective.

▌ Assemble the evidence from the complainant and any supporting evidence he may have. In practical terms this may not be as easy as it sounds. Bullying often takes place in private and work colleagues are usually reluctant to get involved. They may even be part of the problem. This is a case where a chronology would be particularly useful. The complainant may have some diary notes.

▌ Once you have assembled the evidence and assuming there is a case to answer, you will need to conduct a disciplinary interview. The supervisor is not legally entitled to be accompanied to any disciplinary hearing but your policy may require the offer to be made, and in any event, it is best practice. If the supervisor chooses to be accompanied you are advised to have someone accompany you, if only to take notes.

▌ Point out the facts of the alleged misconduct, supported by the documentary evidence, and ask for an explanation. Question him carefully on each element of the allegation and deal with each alleged event in turn. He is unlikely to make a full confession to the allegation but he may make certain admissions, and possibly suggest that there has been a misunderstanding.

▌ Note his reply and inform him that you are to report to the area manager in accordance with your disciplinary policy.

▌ Submit a report with supporting documentary evidence.

▌ The report should contain relevant personal information and any background the discipline officer / senior manager may not be aware of.

These are difficult cases to deal with and often involve different cultures, as discussed in Chapter 3. The evidence gathered during the investigation will dictate what should be done. The outcome could range from words of advice to a final written warning, or if sufficiently serious, dismissal.

Bullying in a workplace is commonplace; the practice can range from overt aggressive and confrontational behaviour to more subtly undermining or ignoring others. It is difficult to deal with but if it is not it can have a disastrous impact on an employee's self-esteem and indeed health. If left unchallenged it can lead to high staff turnover, increased levels of absence, stress-related illness, low morale and unacceptable quality of work.

Of course, as the manager you could consider an alternative approach such as mediation. This is an option but it requires a high level of skill and commitment and may not be acceptable to either party. The new facilities of ACAS could offer mediation in these circumstances.

CASE STUDY 4 – DISCIPLINE

The facts

You are the sales manager in a printing firm. An accounts clerk reports that he suspects that a small number of sales staff have recently begun to submit what he alleges are false expense claims. How would you deal with this?

Options

1. Tell the accounts clerk to mind their own business and that it is your responsibility to manage the sales force.
2. Tell the accounts clerk that the expenses policy is not generous and you allow your staff to make inflated claims to repay them for their hard work.
3. Send a general memo/e-mail to all sales staff informing them that they must ensure that all expense claims are correct, within the company rules and supported by receipts.
4. Pick on one individual, investigate and deal with them as an example to the others.
5. Investigate the allegation and deal with it in a positive manner.

I hope you would take Option 5. Remember that failure to deal with this type of issue, which could amount to criminal activity, could seriously impact on your position within the company. If the matter is minor you could consider Option 3, but as I hope I have stressed before, it is relatively easy to take the right action and then revert to a warning. It is almost impossible to issue the general reminder and then have to take action on the same set of circumstances – the problem would need to arise again. In a similar case I advised on, the accounts clerk was treated as an 'interfering pen-pusher'. The case resulted in a final warning to all the sales team and the dismissal of the sales manager.

Checklist

▌ You must follow your company policy, which may require an investigation by yourself, or better still, the appointment of an independent manager or external consultant. Some policies require the matter to be deal with by financial or audit staff. Unless the amounts are particular high, it would be unusual to report this matter to the police at this stage.

▌ Depending on the severity of the allegation, and of course the impact on the business, the question of suspension should be considered.

▌ Early steps should be made to identify and protect all relevant documents, receipts or IT-based evidence. It is a fact of life that once financial investigations begin, documentary evidence and computer files can disappear.

▌ The investigator should obtain a comprehensive statement from the accounts clerk and any other witness.

▌ A chronology will be particularly useful in a case such as this.

▌ Disciplinary interviews will need to be conducted with each and every suspect and possibly every member of the sales force. These will be complex meetings in which each and every false allegation should be put to the employee.

▌ A comprehensive report should be submitted.

The *points to prove* are the contractual terms or rules relating to expenses and that each suspect was aware of them, possibly by a signed induction checklist or a signed receipt to a copy of the relevant policy. You would need to prove, either by an admission from a suspect or by circumstantial or documentary evidence, that each claim was made knowing it to be false. This may involve checking diaries, client visits, mileage claims, the distance between clients, overnight stays and so on. If the allegations are denied the investigation could be quite detailed. In this case, senior management may wish to use an investigator who understands the accounting system, and of equal importance, has time to devote to the investigation.

You should be aware that if a supervisor or the sales manager signed the expense claims knowing them to be false or without making the necessary checks, this could be treated as gross misconduct, and you should extend your investigation.

If the outcome is that regular and systematic abuse of the expenses system has taken place, it may be practical to prove a selection of the incidents from which to frame the discipline charges.

CASE STUDY 5 – EXTERNAL COMPLAINT OF SEX DISCRIMINATION

The facts

Following the recent recruitment of a replacement personnel manager, your managing director receives a letter from an unsuccessful woman applicant alleging that she was turned down for the post because she had recently married. The letter is passed to you, as an independent manager, for an investigation and report.

The letter contains the following specific allegations:

> I recently applied for the post of personnel manager with your company. I attended an assessment centre with three other candidates and underwent a series of tests and an interview. I was informed yesterday that I was not successful. I sought feedback and was told by the panel chairman, Julian West, that I did not score as high as the successful candidate.
>
> There were two men and a women applicant in her 50s; I understand a male applicant was chosen.
>
> I know from speaking to the candidates at the time that I was the most highly qualified. I have a first degree, an MA in Human Resource Development, I am a member of the CIPD and I have significant experience.
>
> During the interview, one of your directors, Mrs Jones, noted that I had recently married. She asked me whether my husband and I had any plans to have a family. I replied 'Not at this stage.'
>
> I can only assume that my failure to be successful was that your company did not want the risk of me taking maternity leave in the near future. This is discriminatory, and before taking further action, I would like an explanation.

Options

1. Treat the letter as 'sour grapes' and ignore it.
2. Inform the unsuccessful candidate that the best applicant was chosen, it was nothing to do will her gender or recent marriage, and wish her well in finding a suitable position elsewhere.
3. Acknowledge receipt of the letter and inform her that an investigation will be undertaken. It may be appropriate to set a deadline for the reply and inform the complainant accordingly. A senior manager should be appointed to investigate and report.

I hope you would take Option 3. This is a serious complaint, and unfortunately not uncommon on grounds of gender, race, disability and recently age (too young or too old). This type of complaint can arise from an internal, or as in this case an external, source.

It is unlawful for anyone to discriminate against a person in the arrangements made for the purpose of determining who should be offered that employment. In addition to this, the employer is legally responsible for any discriminatory action by an employee. It is essential that a complaint of this nature should be fully investigated.

Checklist

▌ This is a serious allegation which, while it could be false, a misunder-standing, or malicious, might be substantiated. Appoint someone to investigate, ideally someone who understands recruitment and discrimination practice (not, of course, someone involved in the recruitment process complained of).

▌ The investigator may need to interview the complainant if insufficient detail is contained in the letter of complaint. If this is done the investigator would be well advised to be accompanied.

▌ Obtain the recruitment project file and all the relevant interview questions, interview notes, test scores and so on. It is my experience that, even when detailed procedures are set out, interview notes are often incomplete, unreadable and frequently unsigned. Do not, as the investigator, be party to 'putting the file right'. It might backfire on you.

▌ To what extent did the process follow your recruitment policy and procedure, if such a document exists? What were the scores on each element of the assessment? Was the correct decision made? Was the alleged statement about family intentions made, if so by whom, and what were the precise words? If the statement was made, was it corrected at the time (for example by any HR staff present at the interview) and did it colour the judgement or decision? If the scores in each element of the process clearly indicated the superiority of the selected candidate, so much the better. If the process was not properly prepared or recorded, there may be problem.

▌ Interview all of the panel members and obtain statements.

▌ Submit a full report together with all the relevant statements and documents.

▌ The employer will need to frame an appropriate response based on the investigation. There may be a need to review recruitment processes, and possibly for interviewing and equal opportunity training.

▌ The option will always rest with the complainant to resort to litigation if she wishes. However, a thorough investigation will be helpful in preparing a defence.

This is an extremely difficult case and could result in a claim being made. It would, in most instances, be impossible to rectify as an appointment has probably been made. I have included it to show how complex and diverse investigations can be.

CASE STUDY 6 – THEFT

The facts

You are a manager in a local authority. A security guard stops an employee leaving your complex with some stationery materials in a rucksack. The material consists of paper, notebooks, pens, blank computer discs and so on, amounting to around £40 in value. The employee is suspended by the head of her department, in accordance with the relevant policy. The next day you are asked by a director to conduct an investigation. You are informed that a decision has already been made not to inform the police at this stage.

Options

In this scenario you have little option other than to commence the investigation. The option to take no action has, correctly, already been made.

This seems to be a relatively simple issue at the outset but remember the outcome could be a dismissal so the investigation needs to be thorough, effective and fair.

Checklist

▯ The first step is to obtain the relevant policies and procedures relating to the case, such as discipline and searching.
▯ A full statement should be taken from the security guard, describing the circumstances, and what aroused suspicion – was it a random check, a result of someone seeing the goods being taken or an anonymous tip-off? What are the guard's instructions regarding checks on staff?
▯ Obtain precise details such as: what was found, where, and how was it stored? Was it hidden? What was said and by whom at the time the check was made and the goods found? What was the explanation, if any, given by the employee at the time?
▯ Investigate the employee's workplace. Where was the goods taken from? What are the procedures for obtaining stationery?
▯ Are there any other witnesses to the alleged theft or to the search?
▯ Only when you have all the available evidence should you arrange to see the suspended employee. This should be in accordance with the policy, and the employee should be given the opportunity to be

accompanied. If the employee is accompanied the investigator should take someone to take notes.

▌ Prepare your questions beforehand. You might receive a confession. If so, make sure it is written down and signed. If the theft is denied, there might be certain admissions. For example she could hardly deny having the goods unless she alleges they were 'planted' in her bag.

▌ Although this is not a criminal investigation as such, it is important that it is carried out fairly. The standard of proof in discipline cases has already been explained; it is far less demanding than for a criminal prosecution. However, it is good practice to include evidence other than any confession or admission.

▌ The report, statements and so on should be submitted for a decision and discipline hearing.

While a case such as this may be subject to a casual investigation and summary dismissal for gross misconduct in a small business (and this would be fine if an appeal was offered), a large organization is required to follow the full procedure. As previously explained, the law does recognize the limited resources available to a small employer. However, the requirements of reasonableness, fairness and consistency need to be followed in every case.

From a practical point of view, allegations of low-level theft can escalate in allegations such as 'Everyone does it,' 'No one seemed to bother so I just did what the others did,' or 'It was going to be thrown away.' These do not amount to defences to the allegations but they raise questions over what to do next. Your report might contain a separate section on processes within stationery stores and security procedures.

The *points to prove* are relatively straightforward. The goods came from the company stores, they were found in the suspect's possession in suspicious circumstances, and the employee had no authority to possess the goods other than in the workplace. The circumstances would be sufficient to make the assumption that she took them unless she could reasonable establish otherwise.

GENERAL COMMENTS

I could have chosen several other scenarios and some have been mentioned in the book. Typical cases include:

▌ Bar staff 'double-dipping' spirit optics, failing to charge friends or failing to record payments. This may be highlighted by stock deficiencies but would need to be proved against the individual to the standard of reasonable belief. If the theft – for that is what it is – can be isolated to a small number of staff and it cannot be positively established which one or ones were responsible, an employer could discipline and dismiss all the staff in that group. Case law dictates that, provided a reasonable investigation has taken place, this is lawful. It would not, of course, be enough for a criminal prosecution. To be honest, I would feel a little uncomfortable in taking this course of action. I would much rather continue the investigation until a suspect could be identified.

▌ Drinking or taking drugs while at work, or attending work under influence of drink or drugs. This is a difficult scenario and the employer may feel it has some responsibility to take a 'caring' position. Remember, start off in a discipline mode, and if the circumstances merit it, revert to welfare.

▌ Using company vehicles for private purposes. Again, some companies allow this with permission and some do not. The first issue is whether the company insurance allows such use. It might not, and this could leave the employer liable for road traffic offences.

▌ Insubordination and/or refusal to obey reasonable instructions. This is fairly straightforward but you will need to bear in mind the culture of the organization and the need to be consistent.

▌ Running private businesses on company time and IT networks. I have dealt with several of these, such as employees running market gardens and semi-professional entertainers. There are two issues for an employer to consider. First, do you have a clear policy preventing this action? Have your included the fact that monitoring will take place, and do you or your managers in fact carry out the monitoring? Second, does the business activity operate in competition to your own business?

The basis principles are:

▌ Make sure you have the policies and procedures in place to deal with this type of issue.
▌ Before taking any action prepare and plan.
▌ Act fairly and consistently.
▌ Reflect on your performance and progress after each and every stage of an investigation, report, hearing and decision.

14

Pro forma documents

This chapter contains a series of common letter precedents you may find useful. They can all be amended to suit the particular circumstances.

Table 14.1 Pro forma documents

No.	Title	Comments
1	Terms of reference	Various scenarios are shown
2 and 3	Suspension letters	Two versions
4	Statement – optional	Suggested heading and footer
5	Notice of Disciplinary Hearing	
6	Dismissal Letter	Outcome of hearing
7	Not Proven letter	Outcome of hearing
8	Written Warning Letter	Or final warning
9	Notice of Appeal Hearing	
10	Result of Appeal Hearing	With options
11	Capability 1	Invoking formal procedures × 2
12	Capability 2	Written / final warning
13	Capability 3	Dismissal and appeal notice

1   TERMS OF REFERENCE

A   On Friday 24 June 2007, a routine check was made of the company-owned laptops in the sales office. On the laptop allocated to Peter XXX a quantity of indecent images were found saved to the hard drive. Please investigate this matter and report whether any disciplinary action should be taken against this employee. The laptop has been seized by IT and is available in their office. Peter XXX has not been suspended at this stage.

A relatively clear task but carrying the potential to move into several associated areas. If I was not an IT professional I would seek to get the services of such a person for some of the enquiries and technical work.

B   To Joan Clarke, finance manager.

Information has been received that members of the field sales team may have submitted false expense claims.

Please conduct a preliminary investigation and report to the sales director on the nature of any fraud, those involved or suspected, the possible charges and whether any staff should be suspended.

On receipt of this report you may be required to conduct a complete investigation with a view to disciplinary proceedings.

This is an open-ended investigation which could mushroom into a major enquiry. My concern would be whether I could commit the time and effort that it seems to need if I had another section to run.

C   On 21 February 2006 Mrs Veronica XXX (40), computer centre supervisor based at xxx made an allegation of sexual harassment between December 2005 and February 2006 against James XXX (55), senior manager – information technology, based at XXX. Mr XXX is the line manager of Mrs XXX.

Mr XXX was seen by the human resources manager and a director, John Brown, at 3.00 pm on 21 February 2006. He was suspended from duty and served with the attached letter.

You are asked to conduct an investigation into this matter and report to the director, John Brown, who will act as disciplinary officer. A copy of the discipline policy is attached.

This investigation should be conducted in confidence and completed as soon as possible.

This is a case of sexual harassment in which a suspension decision has already been made by the discipline officer. I would wish to be accompanied when I interviewed the complainant, especially as a male investigator.

Notes

I have listed a few of the more obscure terms of reference. A more common one could be 'John Brown and Peter Green were suspended after fighting in the goods yard. Please investigate and report on any proposed disciplinary action.' Or 'The attached grievance letter has been received from Mary Green, a part-time employee, to the effect that she has been refused access to the IT training being provided to all full-time staff. Please investigate and report in order to enable me to answer this grievance.'

Whatever the task you are called to investigate, try to develop into a reflective practitioner – and good luck.

2 EXAMPLE – SUSPENSION LETTER

Dear XXX,

I write to confirm our meeting of today regarding the complaint about your behaviour on 1 April 2008 and your suspension from work. It is alleged that you swore at a cleaner, Mrs Susan Spencer, and threw her cleaning materials across the office. It is also alleged that you accused the cleaner of stealing property from your desk. It is also alleged, and supported by witnesses, that you had been drinking.

The action complained of, if proven, would constitute gross misconduct under the company disciplinary policy. The decision has been taken to suspend you from duty on full pay from the date of this letter, until this matter has been fully investigated and a decision taken regarding the complaint. The investigating manager will be Mary Brown of the sales department.

In order for your account of the incident to be taken, you will be required to attend a discipline interview, the date and time of which will be arranged shortly. You are entitled to be accompanied at that meeting by a trade union representative or a work colleague.

Your suspension is not an indication of guilt, but it is in accordance with the disciplinary procedure. Your suspension will be reviewed on completion of the investigation.

During the course of this suspension you will not be allowed on the company premises, nor should you make contact with any member of staff. You contact with the company will be Keith Clarke, HR manager.

Yours sincerely

Director

3   EXAMPLE – SUSPENSION LETTER

Personal and confidential

Dear XXX,

I am writing to confirm the decision given verbally to you at the meeting on time/date held following the receipt of (a) serious allegation(s) regarding your conduct at work. At the meeting I informed you that you would be suspended from duty, on full pay, as of that date in accordance with the disciplinary procedure laid down in the Discipline Policy (copy attached).

The allegation(s) against you is/are as follows.

(i) It is alleged that you have ... at ... on ... in ....

In view of the seriousness of this/these allegation(s), which could amount to serious misconduct if substantiated, I have decided that an investigation will be carried out. The investigating manager will be XXX.

Subject to the outcome of the investigation, a formal disciplinary hearing may be convened to consider the above allegation(s). You will remain suspended from duty, on the appropriate rate of pay, until the investigation has been completed, and if a hearing is necessary, until the outcome of the meeting is decided.

During the period of your suspension, which does not constitute disciplinary action, you may not enter company premises, contact other staff members or use any of the facilities of the company without prior permission. [State any other conditions, eg hand in keys, security passes, equipment, papers.]

Due to the serious nature of the allegations I have to advise you that, if this/these allegation(s) should be substantiated you could be summarily dismissed from your post without notice.

During your period of suspension all contact with the company should be via Mrs Joan Smith, HR manager. Please contact her if you have any queries about this matter.

Yours sincerely,

4   WITNESS STATEMENT

**CONFIDENTIAL
STATEMENT FORM**

Heading

(Witnesses shall be reminded before making their statements that their evidence could be made available to the employee under investigation.)

Employee's name   _____

Position/job   _____

Date   _____

Place   _____

Times   _____

Persons present   _____

Investigating Officer   _____

Witness   _____

INSERT STATEMENT HERE

Footer

This statement is true. I have been told I can add, alter or amend anything I wish. I have made this statement of my own free will.

Name of witness _____ Date _____

Signature _____

Investigating Officer _____ Date _____

Signature _____

Note: A similar format could be used to record interview notes.

5 EXAMPLE – NOTICE OF A DISCIPLINARY HEARING

Dear XXX,

The investigation into the complaint by Mrs Spencer is now complete. Copies of the documents relating to this case are attached, including agreed facts and admissions together with statements by Mrs Spencer and witnesses to the incident, Mr Jones and Mrs Clarke.

I am writing to inform you that you are required to attend a disciplinary hearing at my office on 16 June 2008 at 11.00 am. At the hearing, I will consider the allegation that you swore at a cleaner, Mrs Susan Spencer, and threw her cleaning materials across the office, the allegation that you accused the cleaner of stealing property from your desk, and the allegation that you had been drinking.

The allegations if proven would amount to gross misconduct under the company's disciplinary procedure, and could therefore result in your dismissal.

You are entitled, if you wish, to be represented at the hearing by a work colleague or a trade union representative. [or 'I have sent a copy of this letter to your trade union representative.'] Your suspension from duty will continue until the disciplinary process has been completed.

Yours sincerely

Director

6 EXAMPLE – DISMISSAL LETTER

Dear XXX,

I write to confirm the outcome of the disciplinary hearing on 16 June 2008 in my office.

The allegations were that on 1 April 2008 you that you swore at a cleaner, Mrs Susan Spencer, and threw her cleaning materials across the office, that you accused the cleaner of stealing property from your desk, and that you had been drinking. You denied all three allegations.

After considering the evidence, I am satisfied that the allegations are true and substantiated. In view of this I reached the conclusion that you have been guilty of gross misconduct and you were therefore summarily dismissed from employment, without notice, with effect from 16 June 2008. You will be paid up to and including 16 June 2008.

You have the right to appeal against this decision, and if you wish to do so, this appeal should be made in writing to the managing director within 10 days.

Yours sincerely

Director

7   EXAMPLE – 'NOT PROVEN' LETTER

Dear XXX,

I write to confirm the outcome of the disciplinary hearing on 16 June 2008 in my office.

The allegations were that on 1 April 2008:

a) you swore at a cleaner, Mrs Susan Spencer, and threw her cleaning materials across the office,
b) you accused the cleaner of stealing property from you desk, and
c) you had been drinking.

You denied all three allegations.

After considering the evidence, I am satisfied that the allegations a) and b) were unfounded. In addition, I reached the conclusion, after hearing the evidence and your submission, that allegation c) was unsubstantiated.

In view of this you were reinstated with immediate effect and no further action will be taken against you in respect of these matters. This matter will not be placed on your personal file.

Yours sincerely

Director

8   EXAMPLE – 'FINAL WARNING' LETTER

Dear XXX,

I write to confirm the outcome of the disciplinary hearing on 16 June 2008 in my office.

The allegations were that on 1 April 2008:

a) you swore at a cleaner, Mrs Susan Spencer and threw her cleaning materials across the office,

b) you accused the cleaner of stealing property from your desk, and

c) you had been drinking.

You denied all three allegations.

After considering the evidence, I am satisfied that the allegations a) and c) were unsubstantiated. In addition, I reached the conclusion, after hearing the evidence, that allegation b) was substantiated.

In view of the fact that you belatedly apologized and of Mrs Spencer's kind remarks, my decision was to give you a written warning, and this letter is in confirmation of that decision. This warning will be placed on your personal file but will be disregarded for disciplinary purposes after a period of one year.

You were reinstated with immediate effect.

You have the right to appeal against this decision, and if you wish to do so, this appeal should be made in writing to the managing director within 10 days.

Yours sincerely

Director

9   EXAMPLE – NOTICE OF APPEAL HEARING LETTER

Dear XXX,

You have appealed against the written warning/final written warning/notice of dismissal confirmed to you in writing on 16 June 2008.

Your appeal will be heard by Dr Judith Smithers, managing director, in her office at 12 noon on 20 June 2008.

You are entitled to be accompanied by a work-based colleague or trade union representative.

The decision of this appeal hearing will be final and there is no further right of review.

Yours sincerely

Human resources manager

10 EXAMPLE – NOTICE OF RESULT OF APPEAL HEARING

Dear XXX,

You appealed against the decision of the disciplinary hearing held on 16 June 2008 that you be given a warning/be dismissed in accordance with the company's discipline procedure. The appeal hearing was held on 20 June 2008. I sat as chair and I was accompanied by a fellow director, Peter Lord.

I am now writing to confirm the decision taken by Jane Smith, the director who conducted the appeal, that the decision to dismiss you without notice stands/the decision to be revoked [specify if no disciplinary action is being taken or what the new disciplinary action is].

You have now exercised your right of appeal under the discipline procedure and this decision is final.

Yours sincerely

Chair of appeal hearing

A SERIES OF LETTERS RELATING TO CAPABILITY

11 EXAMPLE LETTER – NOTICE OF DECISION TO INVOKE THE FORMAL PROCEDURES

Confidential

Dear XXX,

I am writing to inform you that after the company has provided appropriate training, advice and support, your conduct/performance is still unsatisfactory. I have therefore decided to formally invoke the capability procedure, a copy of which is attached.

You are entitled, if you wish, to be accompanied by a work-based colleague or trade union representative at any stage in these formal procedures.

Yours sincerely

Manager

12 EXAMPLE LETTER – NOTICE OF INITIAL REVIEW MEETING

Dear XXX,

I am writing to tell you that you are required to attend an initial/review meeting at time/date/location.

At this meeting the question of formal proceedings being brought against you in accordance with the capability procedure will be considered.

You are entitled, if you wish, to be accompanied by a work-based colleague or trade union representative.

Yours sincerely

Manager

13   EXAMPLE LETTER – NOTICE OF WRITTEN WARNING OR FINAL WRITTEN WARNING

Dear XXX,

You attended a formal hearing on time/date.

I am writing to confirm the decision taken that you be given a written warning/final written warning under the first/second/third stage of the capability procedure.

This warning will be placed in your personal file but will be disregarded for these purposes after a period of [period] months and expunged from the records provided your performance reaches a satisfactory level.

a) The nature of the unsatisfactory performance was […].

b) The performance improvement expected is […].

c) The timescale within which the improvement is required is […].

d) The likely consequence of further misconduct or insufficient improvement is [a final written warning/dismissal].

You have the right of appeal against this decision, in writing, within 10 days of receiving this letter.

Yours sincerely

Manager

14 EXAMPLE LETTER – CONFIRMATION OF DISMISSAL (FOLLOWING PREVIOUS WARNINGS)

Dear XXX,

On [date of last stage letter] you were informed in writing that you would be given a final written warning in accordance with Stage [2/3] of the capability procedure. In that letter you were warned that if your performance did not improve, you were likely to be dismissed.

At the hearing held on [time/date] it was decided that your performance was still unsatisfactory and that you will be dismissed.

I am therefore writing to you to confirm the decision that you be dismissed in accordance with Stage [2/3] of the capability procedure and that your date of termination will be [date]. The reasons for your dismissal are […].

You will be paid up to [date] and your final salary payment will include [period] weeks' pay in lieu of notice.

You have the right of appeal against this decision, in writing to the managing director, within 10 working days of receiving this decision.

Yours sincerely

Manager

References

Buzan, T (1993) *The Mind Map Book*, BCA, London

Gibbons, M (2007) *Better Dispute Resolution – A Review of Employment Dispute Resolution in Great Britain*, DTI, London

Kolb, D (1984) *Experiential Learning Experience as the Source of Learning and Development*, Prentice Hall, New Jersey

Wallington, P (ed) (2007) *Butterworths Employment Law Handbook*, LexisNexis Butterworths, London

WEBSITES

ACAS: www.acas.org.uk

Commission for Equality and Human Rights (CEHR): www.equalityhumanrights.com

Information Commissioner: www.ico.urg.uk

Terrence Higgins Trust: www.tht.org.uk

Index

absence management   41
  ACAS   9
  code of practice   3, 62
  account, peace interviews
      141–43
active listening   134
administration of an appeal   171
administration, disciplinary
      hearings   163–64
admissibility   104–05
admissions   148–50
age discrimination   90
aggressive, disparaging or stress
      question   136
agreed facts or admissions   157
alcohol and drugs   92–94
ambiguities   155
anonymous witnesses   132–33
apologies   55
appeal decisions   171–72

behaviour, meaning of   25

best evidence rule   106
blogs and social network sites
      100
body language   120
breach of contract   69
bullying   86–87, 180–82
Burchell test   108
burden of proof   106–08, 128
  discrimination cases   88–89,
      107–08
Buzan, Tony, mind-mapping   123

capability   72–83
  and disability   83
  checklist   76–79
  dismissal letter   205
  procedure notification letter
      202
  review meeting letter   203
  written or final warning letter
      204
  borderline cases   75

initial action   74–75
case studies   174–89
    bullying   180–82
    false expenses claim   183–84
    sex discrimination   184–86
    sexual harassment   178–80
    simple discipline   175–77
    theft   187
change and change management
    6
changes in work techniques
    79–80
checklist, capability   76–79
    capability dismissal   82
    disciplinary hearing   164–66
    formal discipline   44
    interview   147
    investigator's competencies
        119
    problem solving   122–23
    report format   156
    statements and interview notes
        147–48
    suspension   63
chronology   110–13, 124–25
circumstantial evidence   104
closed questions   136
closure   143
cognitive interviewing   142
collective grievances   47
Commission for Equality and
    Human Rights   84
communication   121–22, 134–35
competencies of the investigator
    119
complaints v grievances   47
compromise agreement   68–69
concepts of report writing
    154–55
conduct outside work   44–46
confessions   148–50
constructive dismissal   68, 181

contract of employment   26
    data protection   97
contrast effect   138
conversation management   142
Corporate Homicide Act 2007   4
corporate manslaughter   4
corroboration   103–04
criminal offences – organizational
    options   90–92
custodial sentence   46
custom and practice   127–28
CV fraud   129

Data Protection Act 1998   95
    principles   95–96
    employers duties   96
    right of employees   97–98
data subject access request   97
deciding to involve the police
    90–91
decision-making   168
detriment   60, 86
difficult conversations   33–35, 74
direct discrimination   86
direct evidence   102–03
disability and capability   83
    discrimination   88
disciplinary hearing   21, 162–70
    appeals   170–72
    hearing notice, example   196
    interview   20, 145–47
    officer   21, 162–63
    panel   163
    reports   153
disclosure, qualifying and
    protected   58
discrimination
    direct   86
    indirect   86
dismissal   72–73
dismissal in capability cases,
    checklist   81–83

dismissal letter, example 197
documentary evidence 106
documents and exhibits 160
drafting a chronology 110–13
driving licence, loss of 94

early complaint in sexual cases 105–06
effective listening 134–35
e-mail misuse 99
employee, meaning of 5
employment protection rights 29, 43
Employment Rights Act 1996 72
engage and explain 141
Equal Pay Act 1970 52
evaluation 143–44
evidence and evidence gathering 101–13
evidence gathering 87, 110
 admissibility 104–05
 circumstantial 104
 definition 101
 direct 102
 documentary 106
 hearsay 105
 indirect 104
 IT 109
 opinion 105
 weight 104–05
external investigators 117
extraneous issues 161

failure to comply with instructions/orders 92
fair dismissal 72–73
final warning letter, example 199
first impression effect 138
fixed term contract 11
follow-up to discipline 172
formal discipline, checklist 44
format of a report 156

forward planning 121
fraud investigations 128–29
fraud preventative measures 128
fundamental attribution error 138

general fitness for work 93
Gibbons review 16
grapevine, managing the 69–70
grievance procedure, drafting 49
 appeals 56
 during discipline investigation 53
 informal resolution 50
 investigations 51–52
 meeting 53
 record keeping 57
 written response 54
gross misconduct 15
 reacting to 43–44
grounds for an appeal 170

harassment 85–86
health and safety 4
hearsay evidence 105
HIV and AIDS 89
Human Rights Act 1998 84, 95, 99

independent witnesses 144
indirect discrimination 86
indirect evidence 104
induction 26, 74
Information Commissioner 97
internal managers as investigators 116–17
internet misuse 99
interview checklist 147
interviewing 130–51
investigator 21, 116
investigators' skill set 117–23
investigator's tools 124
IT evidence 109

job description 26

knowledge, meaning of 24
Kolb's learning cycle 118

leading questions 135
Linford guidelines for anonymous
    witnesses 132–33
loss of driving licence 94

managing relationships 121–22
managing the grapevine 69–70
mind-mapping 123, 153
mirroring 137
misconduct 14–15
    reacting to 41–43
misuse of telephone, e-mail or
    internet 99
mitigating factors or circumstances
    158, 159–61
modified procedure 12, 57
monitoring and surveillance
    97–98
multiple questions 136

negative information bias 138
negative statements 132
negotiation 150–51
no comment replies 142, 145
nonverbal techniques 134
not proven letter, example 198
note-taking v statement writing
    147
notice of appeal letter, example
    200

open question 136
opinion evidence 105
organizational review 61

peace process of interviewing
    139–44

personal data 6
personal mitigation 160
persuading an employee to resign
    68
plain English 154
plan and prepare 139–141
plea-bargaining 161
points to prove 109 125–26, 177,
    184, 188
Police and Criminal Evidence Act
    1984 (PACE) 91
police involvement 90–91
policies and procedures 23
pornography 99, 109
potentially fair dismissal 72–73,
    94
presenting the discipline case
    166–67
presumptions 109
priority setting 121
proactive discipline 7, 22–36
probation 28, 28–30
probing sequence 136
problem solving cycle 122–23
problems in disciplinary hearings
    169–70
promotion and inadequate
    performance 80–81
protecting evidence 126
Protection of Harassment Act 1977
    87
psychometric testing 25
Public Interest Disclosure Act 1998
    58

qualifications 25
question, aggressive, disparaging
    or stress 136
    closed 136
    leading 136
    multiple 136
    open 136

questioning techniques   135–37

race discrimination   88
reactive discipline   7
reasonable adjustments   88
reasonable belief   109, 126, 168
recommendations   159
recording interviews   150
recruitment and selection   24
redundancy   11, 72
references   25
reflective practice   116, 118–20,
   131, 135, 144, 170, 173
reintroduction, after suspension
   70–71
relevant disciplinary action   10
religious belief, discrimination
   89
report writing   152–61
resignation during suspension or
   investigation   67
responsibilities during suspension
   66
result of appeal letter, example
   201
retirement   11, 72
retracting a statement   131–32
return to work interviews   41
right to be accompanied   17–19,
   53
role of the representative
   167–68

secret investigations   115
self-organization   121
sex discrimination   87
sign-posting   166
silence   134–35, 145
similar-to-me   137
situational mitigation   160
skills, meaning of   25
small employer   19–20

some other substantial reason
   (SOSR)   46, 72
standard of proof   90, 94, 108–09
starting the report   157
statement or notes checklist
   147–48
statement writing v note-taking
   147
stereotypes   138
substantiated, meaning of   159
summarizing and rephrasing
   134
suspects   145–47
suspension   62–71
suspension letter, examples
   193–94
suspension procedures   65
   checklist   63

techniques of report writing
   155
telephone misuse   99
terms of reference   123–24, 157,
   191–92
third-party harassment   87,
   179–80
time management   120–22
tools of the investigator   124
trade union representatives   95
traditional interviewing   137–38
training, management   32
tricks and devices   126–27

unfounded, meaning of   158
unstructured interview   137
unsubstantiated, meaning of
   158
using your chronology   124–25

vicarious liability   4
victimization   86, 179
vulnerable witness   145

WASP interviewing technique
    138–39
whistleblowing   58–61
  investigations   60
witness statement, form   195

witnesses   144–45
  independent   144
  vulnerable   145
worker, meaning of   5